EXPERTS PRAISE
Heaven Talks
to Children

"*Fascinating . . . I encourage everyone to open up their hearts and minds to what the purest littlest ones are telling us.*"
— MSGR. THOMAS HARTMAN, co-host of TV's
"The God Squad," co-author of *Religion for Dummies*

"*Extraordinary . . . Heaven Talks to Children is a wealth of information for parents, counselors, and anyone who provides support for the bereaved or wishes to help children understand the many ways that love is the best resource for healing.*"
— LOUIS E. LAGRAND, Ph.D., CT, author of *Love Lives On*

"*An inspiration . . . This collection of children's experiences of heavenly communications will be a blessing to the reader.*"
— REV. HOWARD STORM, author of *My Descent into Death*

"*Truly amazing . . . At last, a really sincere book that will give you many answers and open your mind to the spiritual world of children.*"
— JOSEPH WRIGHT, author of *The Psychic Hypnotist*

"Exceptional, important . . . This book will not fail to move you."

—NANCY CLARK, author of *My Beloved:*
Messages from God's Heart to Your Heart

"Heartwarming and brilliant . . . Christine Duminiak takes us on a compelling journey no other book on childhood afterlife communication can match."

—JOSIE VARGA, author of *Visits from Heaven*

"Invaluable . . . This book provides a great service for parents and the paranormal community to help children whose gifts are misunderstood."

—REV. ROBERT BAILEY, Roman Catholic priest and
co-founder of the Paranormal Warriors of St. Michael

"Educational, moving . . . Heaven Talks to Children *takes you through a journey of love, faith, and courage."*

—JENNY STEWART, founder and director of
Paranormal Research and Resource Society

Heaven Talks to Children

AFTERLIFE CONTACTS, SPIRITUAL GIFTS, AND LOVING MESSAGES

Christine Duminiak

CITADEL PRESS
Kensington Publishing Corp.
www.kensingtonbooks.com

CITADEL PRESS BOOKS are published by

Kensington Publishing Corp.
119 West 40th Street
New York, NY 10018

All Kensington titles, imprints, and distributed lines are available at special quantity discounts for bulk purchases for sales promotions, premiums, fund-raising, educational, or institutional use. Special book excerpts or customized printings can also be created to fit specific needs. For details, write or phone the office of the Kensington special sales manager: Kensington Publishing Corp., 119 West 40th Street, New York, NY 10018, attn: Special Sales Department; phone 1-800-221-2647.

CITADEL PRESS and the Citadel logo are Reg. U.S. Pat. & TM Off.

First printing: August 2010

10 9 8 7 6 5 4 3 2 1

Printed in the United States of America

Library of Congress Control Number: 2010924996

ISBN-13: 978-0-8065-3227-1
ISBM-10: 0-8065-3227-0

To our Heavenly Father, Your Holy Divine Son,
and Your Holy Spirit, I dedicate this book to You.
May this work be pleasing to You and in accordance
with Your holy will and purpose.

Contents

Acknowledgments

I would like to extend my thanks and appreciation to the following people:

To all the contributors to my book who so generously and graciously shared their children's wondrous spiritual experiences to bring more awareness and comfort to others.

To my beloved husband, Bob, whose love and support I cherish. You are a wonderful father and husband and a blessing truly from God.

To our terrific kids, Jamie and Matthew, your dad and I are so very proud of you both. We are so grateful that God entrusted you into our care.

To Sunni Welles, my dearest friend, who has given so generously and freely of her time to answer my many spiritual questions to ensure that my information is as accurate as humanly possible.

To Dr. Louis LaGrand, who gave me sage advice and who patiently critiqued my work.

To Eric Kuzdenyi, a great lawyer and even better friend, who so graciously gave of his free time to give me his learned legal advice.

To Bonnie Fredman, who patiently and meticulously edited all my many miscues.

And last, to Michaela Hamilton, who recognized and believed in the healing value of this book and for making it a reality. What a warm and lovely person you are. It has been a privilege working with you, the best editor-in-chief on the planet. Thank you from the bottom of my heart.

Author's Note

Dear Reader, although I will be using the name Jesus or the God-Christ from time to time in this book, you certainly should feel free to substitute whatever name you personally use, are comfortable with, and is in accordance with your own belief system when referring to your Creator, Divine Source, or Higher Power.

PART I

Visits from Heaven

Can Children Communicate with the Dead?

Have you ever wondered if your child was *really* seeing and talking to the spirit of your deceased mother, father, grandparent, aunt, uncle, sibling, children, pet, angels, or other holy beings, and if so, is this a rare phenomenon?

Have you noticed that your child's ability to see and hear spirits is strongly continuing on through his or her teenage years, and have you been wondering why?

Have you been yearning to guide your child's spiritual gift properly, but didn't know where to even begin? Or have you anxiously wondered if what you've been doing was correct?

Have you been unsure about how to distinguish the difference between a good spirit and a bad spirit, correctly, and how to protect your child safely?

Have you questioned whether your child's supernatural abilities are compatible with your religion? Have you been searching for a book that gives you positive scriptural backup for pursuing spiritual gifts—but have come up empty-handed?

Have you wished that you could find a basic reference guide to explain easily to your younger or older child the mysterious and complex concepts of afterlife contacts, spiritual gifts, death, spirits, angels, Heaven, God, and our life's purpose? Have you been looking for practical advice on how to help your child express and recover from his or her grief?

Congratulations! You have finally found that all-inclusive book on all those many topics in *Heaven Talks to Children*. I believe that you were spiritually led to this book to guide you in finding the answers that your mind and heart have been seeking. This book is that comprehensive, easy-to-understand, basic reference guide. The information included in these chapters will assist you in safely navigating through those uncharted, supernatural, spiritual waters when it comes to afterlife contacts and spiritual gifts. It will be an invaluable blueprint for you better to understand your child's ability to communicate with the spirits. It gives instructions on how to differentiate between good and bad spirits. It gives you simple but powerful protective prayers for you and your children to call upon. It cites specific locations where you can find positive scriptural support to help you feel at peace about using those God-given spiritual gifts. It provides answers to your children's questions on the mystifying topics of death, Heaven, God, angels, spirits, and afterlife visits, and it provides answers to why we are here. It gives thoughtful suggestions on how to assist your grieving child express his or her sad feelings and other emotions and how to recover from the pain of grief.

Most of the world's major religions believe in the existence of God and an afterlife. There are differing beliefs as to what exactly happens after we die and what actually gets us into that wonderful and desired place we call Heaven to be with God for all eternity. Since this is not a book about comparative religions, I have not covered what the major religions' beliefs of the world are on how one can attain Heaven or what other ethereal experiences await us if we do not. There are many books on the market on those topics by very learned and scholarly people.

Although for the purposes of full disclosure, I am an open-minded Catholic with traditional beliefs in the Bible. I also respect those of other faiths and beliefs. However, this book is not going to concentrate on my personal Catholic beliefs, nor is it going to try to convert your own personal belief system to mine. When it comes to the topics of Heaven and our life's purpose, I will be using widespread information gleaned from notable and credible near-death experiences (NDEs), to give you the benefit of fascinating insights into those mysterious topics.

While reading this book, you may come across some spiritual concepts that you do not readily agree with. That is perfectly understandable, of course, and to be expected. If you have been intrigued by these spiritual topics and have done a lot of prior reading on these subjects, you would have probably noticed that not every authority on these matters has identical beliefs. Some very credible authorities on spirituality or religion or both disagree and contradict each other at times, which can be quite confusing to you, the spiritual seeker. Therefore, if you come across some information in this book that you do not agree with, for whatever reason, I respectfully ask that you keep an open mind.

Perhaps you could briefly pray about it, asking God to reveal to you the truth about what you are reading. I also ask that if you do not agree with some of the information in this book, take with you what does feel right to you and store in the back of your mind that which you do not presently agree with. At a later time in your personal spiritual journey, you may be pleasantly surprised to find that the information you questioned may suddenly ring true to you after all. It may be the missing piece of the spiritual puzzle you discover fits in perfectly, giving you that elated aha moment of enlightenment and satisfaction!

I would like to move on and share with you what prompted me to write about children's afterlife encounters by starting off with a strange spiritual occurrence from my own childhood. When I was around six or seven years old, there were a few times when I feared I was going blind. A sudden and unexpected brilliant, white light, shaped in a sphere about one inch in diameter would manifest itself in my mind's eye. This white ball of light would transform itself slowly into a neon purplish color and continue to change into a glowing lime green color. The colors were breathtakingly beautiful. This luminous sphere would be superimposed over physical objects in my direct field of vision. This phenomenon would last for about thirty seconds and then completely dissipate into the same nothingness it mysteriously materialized from. Those thirty seconds, though, felt like an eternity to a scared little kid who thought this episode could possibly mean that she was going to go blind.

The strange light's appearance only happened a few times when I was a child. And I didn't tell my parents or anyone else about it. I was just so relieved that it would always disappear and that my eyesight wasn't affected. So I was happy to put it out of my mind and to continue playing. From my own childhood experiences, I can now identify with those children who have experienced unusual spiritual phenomena and who have never given it a second thought. Children seem to accept things that happen easily, even when they are out of the ordinary. Many times they just keep it close to the vest.

I do not believe in coincidences. So while writing this book in 2009 when two different women contacted me within a few weeks of each other about a similar ball of light, I felt I was meant to share their circumstances with you here. There may be others who have been experiencing this same phenomenon. These two women (who do not know each other) contacted me separately for guidance. They both were experiencing a manifestation of a similar brilliant purple and lime green ball of light. In one woman's case, immediately after the ball of light would materialize, she would start to see visions of future events with precise details concerning the people involved. Some of these future events have since come true. The other woman said she saw a purple and green colored light appear to her in her room. While she was observing it, she felt a sense of her loved one's spiritual presence.

In my particular case, I had forgotten all about the mysterious and colorful brilliant sphere of light that I had occasionally experienced as a child. It was not until a few decades later in 1998 that it would return, and then it was only after an unexpected amazing supernatural visit I received from the afterlife from my in-laws. Although I am neither a psychic nor a medium, on March 19, 1998, my "dead" mother-in-law and father-in-law spontaneously appeared to me in my bedroom during the night, and they stayed for about an hour. This otherworldly visit rocked my world. I had never had an afterlife visit prior to my dead in-laws' appearance on that extraordinary night. This was to be the first of many frequent visits from them.

After the first miraculous appearance of my in-laws in 1998, I started to see a familiar brilliant white sphere of light in my mind's eye that would transform itself into glowing colors of purple and lime green. The appearance of this luminous sphere jogged my memory back in time to my childhood experiences with the same glowing light. It now dawned on me that when I was a young child, the extraordinary light appearing to me was some type of spiritual contact from the other side. I had no way of knowing this at the time.

Now, as an adult, when the luminous ball of light started to appear again, something new had been added to it. I could actually *see* into the light, and I could see a few people standing in the middle of it. They looked like floating silhouetted people who were wearing fedora hats. It was like a portal into the other side. I had a knowingness that these silhouetted figures were my loved ones who were visiting me from Heaven. My heart was overwhelmed with awe, appreciation, and love whenever this would happen.

After the initial apparition of my dead in-laws on March 19, 1998, they continued to appear to me a few times a week. I had no idea why, nor did I know what these frequent afterlife visits could possibly mean. Although my in-laws' apparitions gave me a great deal of peace, I noticed at other times there were other opaque-looking spirits in my bedroom too. I didn't know who they were or why they were there. They made me feel a bit unnerved and vulnerable, and I wasn't in control of my situation. I started dreading going to bed at night, even though my husband was sleeping right beside me.

I contacted the pastor of my church seeking answers and assistance about these apparitions. He was very kind and caring; however, he was not able to shed any new light on what was happening to me spiritually. All he was able to offer was that when he was in the seminary, one of the priests mentioned something about his experiencing a friendly poltergeist. Unfortunately, that was mainly the extent of his knowledge about spirits and apparitions. So I was forced to go outside of my church and my comfort zone to find meaningful answers. I went on an unrelenting quest to learn everything I could about afterlife contacts. I searched the Internet. I watched shows on TV about spirits visiting from the afterlife. I read many books on the subject, anything that I could get my hands on that would educate me and help me feel at ease when those unidentified spirits would show up when I went to bed at night.

For protection, I tried using all the methods that were advised in the numerous books I had read on the subject: I tried visualizing white light around me, and I tried forcefully and firmly talking to the spirits and establishing boundaries with them. However, not all those suggested methods worked for me. Those unidentified spirits just would not leave, although I really wanted them to. I continued to feel so vulnerable. It was so spooky going to bed at night and seeing that I was not alone.

Finally a few different people suggested that I contact Judith Guggenheim, coauthor of *Hello from Heaven* and one of the original researchers in the field of after-death communications (ADCs) in America and Canada. So I did. She recommended that I get in touch with a good friend of hers, Sunni Welles. Welles is an internationally renowned and highly gifted Christian spiritual conduit and prophet.

I followed Guggenheim's prudent advice and had a private session with Welles. In that comforting and life-changing session, it was explained to me that I was not a psychic or a medium, but rather that my in-laws were just visiting to say hello and to help guide me along a certain path in my life. Some of the ways mentioned that I would be helping others would be spiritually, emotionally, and physically, using the gift of touch healing.

Welles also gave me specific prayers to say to protect myself from unwanted spirits that were not of God. The protective prayers she shared with me proved to be the most powerful and effective means of protection that I have ever come across. This was the missing link that finally gave me the peace and empowerment that I had longed and prayed for at night when all types of spirits would show up uninvited. I will be sharing those specific powerful protective prayers with you later on in chapter 6.

The repeated nightly apparitions from my beloved in-laws combined with the information given to me in my session with Welles turned out to be powerful catalysts for my life's new direction. I eventually went into the field of spiritual bereavement support and became a Certified Grief Recovery Specialist. During my bereavement support work, very surprisingly, I was finding that countless numbers of the bereaved, from diverse belief systems, were also receiving ADCs through contacts and signs from their departed loved ones. To my amazement, I discovered that many people actually *expected* to receive an afterlife contact or a sign and were quite distressed when one was not forthcoming. I would frequently hear anguished and desperate pleas for help from the bereaved. They would say that they would never know for certain whether their loved ones were okay unless they received an afterlife sign from them. They would say that without an afterlife sign they would never be able to feel at peace with their passing.

There was one woman in particular named Winnie, whose son Roy had passed. Her profound longing for an afterlife sign especially touched my heart. I found her deep pain and sorrow to be especially gut wrenching, and it prompted me to do something proactive I had never considered doing before.

By now it was the year 2000, and my own beloved father had passed. I felt greatly blessed by God to be receiving many types of comforting afterlife signs from my dad. Receiving those signs turned my own personal sorrow into joy. I was so very grateful to God for allowing my dad to come and visit me in so many beautiful ways and for healing my heart's sorrow that I wanted to pay this feeling forward to help Winnie and the others who were grieving and pleading for an ADC sign.

So in order to assist them, I founded a nondenominational Internet grief support and prayer group called Prayer Wave for After-Death Communication. In 2009 our large and diverse prayer group included close to six hundred members from twenty-one countries around the world. We take prayer requests from those who long to receive an afterlife sign from their loved ones. My website www.christineduminiak.com also offers a safe haven and message board where the bereaved can learn, discuss, and celebrate their afterlife contacts without the fear of ridicule or disbelief that so many encounter when they try to talk to nonbelievers about afterlife contacts. Many grieving hearts have been healed over the years because of God's tender love and mercy by His answering the prayers of this wonderful, compassionate group.

As a result of our Prayer Wave for After-Death Communication group's prayers, an astounding number of bereaved people were finally receiving comforting afterlife contacts from their loved ones. So much so that I believe I was spiritually led to write about their afterlife contacts in a book to share with others. In 2003 I published *God's Gift of Love: After-Death Communications,* which is a compilation of one hundred twenty-three true stories of comforting afterlife contacts from loved ones and which categorizes and describes in detail twenty common types of afterlife contacts and signs.

While writing *God's Gift of Love,* I came across many amazing accounts of children who had seen and heard from the spirits of deceased loved ones, pets, Jesus, and angels. I was fascinated by their innocent accounts of talking to the dead. As time went by, I received spiritual guidance to write another book devoted just to children's spiritual experiences. I followed that heavenly guidance, and I began to delve into this spiritual phenomenon further. I was fascinated to find that children routinely seemed to be naturally inclined to see and hear spirits, much more so than adults. It seems adults were receiving contacts generally through more subtle ways such as dreams, touches, scents, audio, coins, and so on, whereas many children were actually *seeing* and *talking* to spirits while they were awake. Sometimes on a regular basis! It was as if there was no veil or barrier separating their natural and supernatural worlds. Since little children are too young to comprehend our cultural and religious views on death and the afterlife and do not have those adult filters, they innocently "tell it like it is" when they see and hear from a "dead" person.

I was captivated by the nonchalant way young children would often spontaneously blurt out about seeing a dead person, without even knowing that person had died or even understanding the meaning of death. The children fully expected that everyone around them could see that spirit too and would become quite exasperated when others couldn't understand what they were talking about. Children were communicating with spirits and didn't even know they were talking to the dead. It all seemed very ordinary to them. It's become obvious to me that many times those imaginary friends we used to attribute automatically to being make-believe playmates can be more than just make-believe; they can actually be spirits.

I was finding that if a young child's natural God-given spiritual ability to communicate with Heaven is believed, nurtured, encouraged, and accepted and that if taught how to call on God for his or her protection and feelings of safety, then this special gift may continue through the rest of the child's life. This gift could be used for a higher purpose (God's purpose) to bring comfort and greater good. However, if the child was frightened, not believed, ridiculed, made to feel ashamed or odd, then the child could develop certain fears and apprehensions and may decide to turn off to his or her spiritual gift. In that case, my studies reveal that the gift will most probably leave the child around eight to ten years old, if not sooner.

Dr. Lisa Miller, a psychotherapist and also a professor of psychology at Columbia University Teacher's College, advises that some children with spiritual gifts are discriminated against. Miller has met children who were pulled out of their classrooms and isolated from other children after the children told others the spirits of their grandparents had contacted them. Miller has learned that in some countries around the world, for example, India, China, and Mexico, being contacted by one's grandparents is something to be welcomed. The notion that our ancestors would be in touch with us and would do things for us is not only welcomed but crucial, according to Miller's findings.

Although in the United States we have not yet reached that same easy openness and welcoming acceptance as other countries have, I am hopeful that the stories in this book will help change that. The stories in *Heaven Talks to Chidren* are from people of the following religions: Catholicism, Islam, Judaism, and Christianity. Also, others who consider themselves to be metaphysical or spiritual people and say they are not part of any organized religion. Some names have been changed to protect the contributors' privacy, but the facts they reported have not been altered.

There are over one hundred delightful testimonials about children who innocently and excitedly told their parents or their grandparents that they saw and heard from their dead grandfathers, grandmothers, fathers, uncles, aunts, cousins, brothers, sisters, friends, pets, Jesus, and angels. The stories are grouped into three age groups, one to four, five to nine, and ten to seventeen years old. In some cases, the child was born *after* the death of the family member who appeared to them, so he or she never knew that person! In other cases, the very young child had never been told that the person had died, and yet the child was still communicating with the family member as if he or she was still physically here. There are instances where someone who had committed suicide showed the child that he or she was happy and okay now, which helped to deliver a great deal of relief and peace to the suffering surviving family members.

These spiritual experiences were therapeutic and healing for their families. They helped their families know that their loved ones do live on, and that those who are in Heaven continue to see and hear us and try to let us know this by their comforting afterlife visits.

Sometimes God will bless us by sending our departed loved ones to us as a gift of love and compassion, even though we have not prayed or asked for a visit. Many of the children's experiences in this book, however, were as a direct result of prayer from another grieving family member hoping to receive an afterlife sign. It is my learned belief that spirits in Heaven are under the direct and holy authority of God and, like His angels, are loving servants of God. So I believe those spirits, who visit us to console us, have been given license to do so by God, and we shouldn't be afraid of the visit. If you or your child has been comforted by a spiritual visit from a loved one, then the thanks goes to God, who, I believe, is trying to reassure and console you with this gift of love bestowed upon you in your time of mourning.

Children are pure and innocent messengers between Heaven and Earth. Their extraordinary connection is meant to bring us love, comfort, and healing from grief by sharing the wonderful news that our loved ones in Heaven are okay and do drop by for a visit from time to time.

> *Let the little children come to me,*
> *and do not hinder them,*
> *for the kingdom of God belongs to such as these.*
> —MARK 10:14

CHAPTER I

Apparitions of Saints and Others

✥ If you are skeptical about the dead actually having the ability to visit us from the afterlife because you have never heard of this phenomenon or have not personally experienced an afterlife visitation or think that God would never allow an afterlife contact from the dead, then your skepticism is perfectly understandable. You may not be aware that ADC researchers and coauthors of *Hello from Heaven*, Bill and Judith Guggenheim, have stated that it's estimated that 60–120 million Americans (20–40 percent of the population of the United States) have had one or more (spontaneous and direct) ADC experiences.

However, even if your mind cannot fully comprehend it or believe it, I ask that you please be deferential and supportive of those who have had the pleasure of experiencing this type of spiritual phenomenon. Remember, we are limited human beings who do not have absolute knowledge and all the answers to life's biggest mysteries. If you are open minded and respectful to those who bravely share their sacred experiences with you, you may find that in your own time of great sorrow and mourning, God may bless you this way too. Keeping your mind open for all possibilities that are outside of the box of your human understanding can be your master key to opening up your own spiritual door to God and his amazing miracles.

The following is relevant, thought provoking, and encouraging information from credible people on after-death visits for you to consider:

- *The Vatican*—In January 1999 the Reverend Gino Concetti, chief theological commentator for the Vatican newspaper, told the London Observer Service that the Roman Catholic Church believes in the feasibility of the dead being able to communicate with the living because of the Communion of Saints. The Church believes that communication is possible between those who live on this earth and those who live in a state of eternal repose, in heaven or purgatory. Concetti further advised that it may even be that God lets our loved ones send us messages to guide us at certain moments in our life. Concetti's comments were made in support of the very prominent American theologian and author Rev. Richard John Neuhaus who said that a friend of his had seen a ghost. (Neuhaus, who died in January 2009, was an author, an editor in chief of *First Things,* and a leading intellectual who also informally advised President George W. Bush.)

    On a personal note, in 2004 I wrote Neuhaus about his being referenced in this London Observer Service article. I told him about my book and about my wish that more people, including the clergy, were aware of the Roman Catholic Church's positive stance on afterlife contacts. Neuhaus corresponded back to me saying, "It is, of course, important to discern the spirits and to do so carefully, but the Church certainly does not deny the possibility of the communications of which you write."

- *Beliefnet*—In May 2005, Lisa Schneider of Beliefnet.com (the leading multifaith online community for faith and spirituality) in her article "Faith in the Departed" reported her findings from an online survey of 10,000 respondents about ADCs. One of the questions asked was if anyone ever felt that the deceased were ever trying to communicate with them. The survey received more than 3,800 essay responses to this question. Schneider reported that those who responded in the affirmative greatly outnumbered the skeptics. Those of all faiths, even atheists/agnostics, shared testimonials of supernatural encounters.

- *C. S. Lewis*—The popular Christian author C. S. Lewis of *The Chronicles of Narnia* series and the notable author Sheldon Vanauken have both reported seeing the ghosts of their wives, according to Brother John-Paul Ignatius of the Order of the Legion of St. Michael. Ignatius explains in his article *"Seven Types of Ghosts: A Catholic, Biblical Perspective"* that the renowned prolific author Peter Kreeft, Ph.D., mentions this fact in his books.

- *Canonized saints*—Some of the Catholic Church's canonized saints have been reported to have made afterlife apparitions. Canonized saints are considered holy people known for their heroic virtue and through whose intercession three irrefutable miracles are required. These people were only declared saints after years of extensive investigations, testimonials, and documentation. The Church is extremely wary about being fooled by people who make false claims, so they do exhaustive research along each step of the path to sainthood. Patricia Treece, saint expert and top-selling author on spirituality and saints, has thoroughly researched documentation and testimonials about apparitions reported by extremely credible and ordinary people. Some of the people reporting to have received apparitions were later declared saints themselves by the Roman Catholic Church. The following five summarized accounts of after-death ap-

pearances that were reported by Catholic and Jewish people
are from Patricia Treece's book *Apparitions of Modern Saints*:

1. Mother Cabrini (1850–1917) was a teacher and founder
   of an order of nurses, teachers, caretakers, and administra-
   tors. She was an excellent businesswoman who built hos-
   pitals, orphanages, and schools. Once when Cabrini was
   in great need of some immediate assistance, she prayed to
   one of the dead holy nuns of her religious order and asked
   the nun to go to God and obtain the favor for her. That
   same evening, Cabrini heard a gentle knock at her door,
   and then the door opened and in walked the dead nun.
   The nun assured Cabrini there would be a successful reso-
   lution to her problem. She also told Cabrini where she
   could find some important lost documents. All did turn
   out well, as the dead nun had predicted, and the direc-
   tions to the missing papers turned out to be correct too.
   Cabrini was declared a saint of the Church in 1946.

2. Rabbi Herbert Weiner of Temple Sharey Tefilo-Israel in
   South Orange, New Jersey, wrote the book *9½ Mystics:
   The Kabbala Today.* In Weiner's book he writes about personally studying with S. Z. Setzer, an expert in the
   Kabbala and Jewish mysticism. Weiner describes an
   interesting story about Setzer. One of Setzer's sisters had
   become seriously ill. While Setzer was in his room one
   day, his sister suddenly appeared to him. Then he heard a
   voice whisper in his ear that his sister had died. The next
   day he received a telegram that his sister had indeed died.
   He figured out the time of her death to be at the exact
   moment he heard the whispered message.

3. The Italian Franciscan priest Padre Pio, who while alive,
   was a stigmatic and had the supernatural gift of bilocation. (Bilocation is defined as the simultaneous presence

of a person in two different places.) During his life as a priest, Pio had been visited by Jesus, the Blessed Mother, various dead saints, as well as many dead people not known to be saints. After his death in 1968, it has been reported that Pio has visited many people back here on earth, and through his intercession with God, cures were granted to them. In 2002 Pio was officially canonized a saint of the Roman Catholic Church.

4. In 1941 in an Auschwitz concentration camp in Poland, prisoner Francis Gajowniczek, a former Polish army sergeant, was chosen at random to be executed. Gajowniczek cried out for his wife and two children just before they were going to kill him. Hearing Gajowniczek's cries for his family, another prisoner, Father Maximilian Kolbe, stepped up to volunteer to take Gajowniczek's place and was executed in place of Gajowniczek. Almost fifty years later in 1990, Kolbe, who was by then declared a saint by the Catholic Church, appeared to Gajowniczek after Gajowniczek was in an accident and pronounced dead. Gajowniczek was met in the spiritual realms by Kolbe who told him that it was not yet his time. And Kolbe was correct. Gajowniczek lived on to tell about his near-death experience.

5. In 1907, twenty-eight-year-old Sister Teresa Valsé Pantellini was lying ill in the infirmary suffering from terminal tuberculosis when the deceased Don Bosco appeared to her. Don Bosco was the cofounder of her religious order, the Daughters of Mary Auxiliatrix. Don Bosco had died from emphysema when Teresa was only ten years old. Because she had seen many photos of him over the years, she was able to recognize him when he appeared to her.

In the afterlife visitation to Teresa, she noticed that Don Bosco looked very athletic and much younger than in his photos. As he approached her, she immediately stopped him from giving her a cure and asked him to cure Sister Giovanna instead. Giovanna had been seriously ill for years and was lying in the room next door in the infirmary. As it turned out Giovanna had just finished saying her third novena to Don Bosco asking him to pray on her behalf for a cure. Don Bosco appeared to Giovanna very briefly, and as he went to leave, Giovanna started running around her room crying, "I've seen Don Bosco, and I am cured." Giovanna lived for over thirty more useful years. This was a case where both nuns were able to corroborate the supernatural appearance of Don Bosco visiting them the same evening that Giovanna was granted a cure.

After Teresa's death, the Pope bestowed upon her the title of venerable, which is the first step in the process of sainthood. Don Bosco was declared a saint in 1934.

The five preceding remarkable supernatural accounts show that at times God sends to earth known saints and others for the purposes of giving messages, comfort, guidance, and help. Why then would God not also send to us our own family members and friends who are in good standing with God (who are considered informal saints) for the same purposes of aiding and comforting us? The following 108 children's amazing stories may help you to agree!

PART II

The Children's Stories

CHAPTER 2

Afterlife Encounters
Children One to Four Years Old

Children are pure spiritual bridges between Heaven and
Earth. Our loved ones, who are now residing on the other
side in God's paradise, often use the natural openness and the God-
given spiritual abilities of innocent children to send us love, comfort,
and healing, while they are awaiting our joyful reunion. These visits
are a blessing from God. The following fifty-one true stories are delightful and amazing testimonials about children ages one to four
seeing and talking to spirits of loved ones, spirit guides, and angels
and to those who have committed suicide. In a number of cases, the
child identified the "person" as a family member who died before the
child was born. In some cases, the child was too young to understand
that the person had died and emphatically insisted that he or she was
there talking to the person in the room. In some cases, the child remembered talking to the person in Heaven while waiting to be born,
and this person had in fact died before the child was ever born.

The Rainbow Angel

It was a cold, sunny day in January 2002 as I was driving my then
three-and-a-half-year-old daughter Tia to preschool. From out of
nowhere, she astounded me and said, "When is Uncle Ed going to

die? I miss him and I want to see him." I told Tia that I would make plans for her to see him soon.

My Uncle Ed was like a grandfather to me. He and his wife, my Aunt Jeanne, had raised my mother from childhood. We didn't see Uncle Ed a lot, but I knew how much he loved Tia. He had made that apparent ever since he held her in his arms the first day I brought her home from the hospital.

The very next day, after Tia's uncanny question about when was Uncle Ed going to die and her request to see him, Uncle Ed suffered a stroke and his brain was hemorrhaging. We went to visit him in the hospital several times, and thankfully he was lucid during those visits.

However, a little while passed and Uncle Ed's condition worsened. We knew it was only a matter of time before he'd pass on, so he was transferred to a nursing home for end-of-life care. Soon afterward I visited Uncle Ed by myself one morning, with the plan of bringing Tia back with me in the afternoon after she had her nap. When I returned home, I found that Tia wasn't able to sleep because she was very anxious to visit her Uncle Ed. It seemed very important for her to visit him as soon as possible. She insisted on wearing her new pink dress and tights for the occasion.

I remember on the way to the nursing home that eventful day, Tia had asked if we could stop at McDonald's drive-through, so I did. Tia began eating her Happy Meal in the car and carried her unfinished French fries with her as we rode the elevator up to the third floor of the nursing home. As the doors of the elevator opened, I was startled to hear the sound of a loud bell ringing. It was almost deafening. We saw my mother and niece running down the hall frantically in search of a nurse. My heart sank.

When we entered Uncle Ed's room, he was gasping for air and my Aunt Jeanne was fearfully standing by his side. Through our desperation, fears, and tears, we adults were holding him and telling him we loved him. With all the commotion going on in his room, I was worried about Tia. I wondered what she must be thinking and feeling right now as she was witnessing all of this. Would she be traumatized? However, Tia just quietly sat there on a chair dangling her feet in the corner of the room, while happily eating her leftover McDonald's French fries. Amazingly, she seemed unfazed by our raw displays of emotion. Right after these thoughts briefly filled my mind, Uncle Ed passed over.

We were in the midst of comforting my Aunt Jeanne, when I suddenly noticed that Tia was joyfully skipping up and down the nursing home hallway, and she was singing! Her cheeks were bright red, and she was glowing. She was very excitedly telling people that Uncle Ed had died, as if it were cause for a grand celebration! As she continued to rejoice, it finally dawned on me. Uncle Ed was letting us know, through little Tia, that he was with God and joyfully dancing with the angels.

As Tia and I were heading home that evening, I was crying and praying. Tia told me she knew that Uncle Ed was going to die because the angel had told her. I asked her about this angel and wanted Tia to describe her to me. I took notes as she began telling me of an angel with pink hair. All my life, I had believed in angels, but after hearing that this angel had *pink* hair, I dismissed Tia's story as being fantasy.

After putting Tia to bed that night, I was cleaning off the kitchen table and decided to toss my notes about Tia's angel into the trash along with some old amusement park tickets. While discarding those things, I felt a strong sense of guilt, but chose to ignore it. Exhausted from the emotional events of the day and my overwhelming grief, I simply sat down on the floor and cried and prayed for Uncle Ed.

The next morning when I went back into the kitchen, to my shock and bewilderment, lying on the countertop were my discarded notes about Tia's angel and the old amusement park tickets I had thrown away the night before! I felt a deep chill travel up and down my spine. Convinced that this was a heavenly message for me to believe Tia, I asked her to tell me again about this pink angel. She replied, "You mean the Rainbow Angel?"

The words "Rainbow Angel" really grabbed my attention. Uncle Ed's daughter Diane had died several years before, and prior to her passing, she said she would send them a rainbow to let them know that she was okay. Several months after Diane's passing, Uncle Ed and Aunt Jeanne told me about seeing a beautiful rainbow right in the middle of their dark hallway. They knew this rainbow was the heavenly sign promised by their daughter.

Tia shared more with me about the Rainbow Angel. She said the angel had visited her in the car on the way to the nursing home and in the elevator. The Rainbow Angel told Tia that Uncle Ed was going to die, go to Heaven, and watch over her.

Tia said, "I heard her voice in the alligator [elevator], and I thinked [thought] it in my head too. The Rainbow Angel also visited me last night." "Angels are like ghosts; they don't have any skin." She also said, "The angel floats above me and doesn't even crush me."

Periodically, since Uncle Ed's passing, the Rainbow Angel has visited Tia. Tia said she feels joy when she's with the angel. Tia has also said that she doesn't need to use words or her mouth when she talks with the angel. She drew me a crude picture of information being transferred between the angel and herself. Tia has also described and drawn pictures of soul travel. She has told me stories about the Rainbow Angel taking her to Heaven.

When Tia was seven years old, she could still vividly remember all the angel's visits. Tia has said that the angel has brought along other visitors at times, including Uncle Ed (who she says looks younger) and some children. Tia has never been afraid of her experiences.

Tia has not been visited by the Rainbow Angel for a while. Tia cries when we talk about the angel because she misses her so. Tia anxiously awaits her next meeting with the Rainbow Angel.

—*Lisa, Minnesota*

Before I Was Born

My grandson Ethan is a wonderful, bright, loving, and fun-loving child. I love him dearly. I have always felt that he was part of my soul family, and we have definitely hit it off from day one.

I have many family pictures in my home. When Ethan was about four years old, he was in my house, and he was drawn to some pictures on an end table in my living room. I had never talked to him about these particular pictures or about who any of the people were. However, Ethan pointed to both my mother and father in the pictures and told me who they were. I asked him how he knew this because they had both passed on before Ethan was born.

He said his Grandpa Moone (my father) came to him in a dream before he was born and took him for a walk in the woods. He said he saw Grandpa Moone walking along a pathway toward him. He had a large dog with him. He said there were leaves on the ground and there was a huge boulder nearby. There was green grass on the ground, and as I interpreted it, a grove of trees.

The area reminded me very much of where my father used to live in Virginia. This was similar to the view you would see when you looked out of the second story window of my father's house. After asking Ethan more questions, I realized that the large dog with my dad was his beloved German shepherd named Sarge.

Ethan even mentioned that the shirt my father was wearing was a red plaid shirt. In the picture in my living room, my father was not wearing a red plaid shirt. But that red plaid shirt was very significant to me because a red plaid shirt was a favorite shirt of my father's that he often wore in life. Ethan said my father told him that he would be with him always, and that when he was born, he would protect him and teach him.

Ethan also recognized the picture beside my father's as that of Grandmother Moone (my mother, who used to teach children and simply adored them). Ethan has also told me that he has dreams and sees other people in his dreams. I think this frightens him a bit right now, but I have explained some things to him about this to help ease his fears.

In my home there is the spirit of a little boy who looks to be about five years old. I have seen him, and Ethan has too. Ethan sees the little boy when he visits our home, and the little boy likes to be around Ethan. Ethan has seen him ever since we moved into this house three years ago.

Ethan is now six and is very mature for his age. He seems to have a healing gift because sometimes he will lay his hands on his mother and me, and he tells us, "It will help you feel better." And we do! What a wonderful blessing we have in him.

—Monique Moore, Florida

Quit Blowing Spit

Our son Tyler was born full term and healthy on October 6, 2008, at 4:45 P.M. We were sent home from the hospital after our allotted time because the doctors said that everything was fine with my baby. After three days of being home, I noticed he had an abnormal-looking, key-shaped eye, and I immediately called his pediatrician. The pediatrician had no clue as to what was wrong and sent us to an eye specialist. Tyler was diagnosed with having a coloboma in his eye. This is when a portion of a structure of the eye is absent, usually the iris, retina, or the optic nerve. It wasn't considered a major problem and not a health risk, so we left it alone.

I eventually changed pediatricians because the first one hadn't noticed the eye defect or knew what it was when I pointed it out to him. I no longer felt confident in his abilities. Our new pediatrician was terrific. She was knowledgeable, caring, kind, and helpful getting Tyler on track with his required shots. Whenever we had a medical issue, she was able to remedy it.

By the time Tyler was five months old, I had taken him to the ER three times—all having to do with tummy problems that bothered him tremendously. Thankfully, he was just constipated those times. The doctots were able to take care of the problem, but no one said that we were doing anything wrong or that we should be doing anything differently. We believed we were being good and responsible parents.

On March 19, Tyler was happy and playful that morning. He drank his bottle, and we gave him some baby food peaches to eat. He fell asleep on the living room couch, so I put him to bed in my mother-in-law's room. I checked in on him very often in between taking my shower and getting ready for work. Only ten minutes elapsed before my last check-in and right before I was to leave for work. I went to the back room to give him his daily good-bye kiss. Well to my shock and horror, he was simply not here on this Earth anymore. When I touched him, I knew this immediately. I ran for the phone and called 911, while my brother-in-law did emergency CPR on him. Once he was at the ER, the hospital tried everything they could to bring him back. But it was all in vain. They pronounced my son dead at the same time he had entered this world, 4:45 P.M.

Heartbroken, I didn't know how to tell my then three-year-old son Trevor that his baby brother, Tyler, wasn't coming home. Trevor loved him so much. So until I found a way to explain it to Trevor, I simply told him that Tyler was still at the doctor's. I also told Trevor that he needed to go to his aunt's house to stay the night. I had wanted to make funeral arrangements the next day.

I will now share with you the most amazing and extraordinary heavenly visits that my son Trevor received. The night my five-month-old son Tyler passed away was the same night my three-year-old son Trevor told me that Tyler was in the clouds watching us. Now Trevor had only been told that Tyler was still at the doctor's. I looked at him in amazement and bewilderment. The confident look that Trevor gave me was all so comforting and reassuring.

The next day after we were finished making the funeral arrangements, we went to pick up Trevor from his aunt's house. He asked where Tyler was, and I finally told him that Tyler had gone to heaven with Trevor's fish. It was the simplest way I knew to tell him. He nodded and remained quiet for a while before asking me if we could go see Tyler later on that day. I told him not yet, but we'll get to see him sleeping one more time before we close his box and put him in the ground like we did his fish.

He again looked at me as though he understood but was still a little puzzled. He asked quickly yet confidently, "But can't we talk to him from here?" At that moment I felt a shiver go over my body and looked down at Trevor's hands. He was holding something in his right hand.

I asked, "Why are you holding your hand like that?"

He said, "Tyler is holding my finger and won't let go."

I wanted to cry right then so badly, but didn't want to upset Trevor. I hugged him tightly and told him that he could talk to Tyler whenever he wished.

That night I took him by the hand and we walked outside. I showed him the moon and stars and told him that if he ever wanted to talk to Tyler, that he could just look up to the moon, stars, sun, and clouds and see his brother and talk to him. Shockingly, he then let me know that Tyler was not up in the sky, but was sitting on the ground beside us, and that Tyler had told him to tell Daddy and me not to cry on Monday. Trevor then asked me what would happen on Monday. I told him about the plans for Tyler's burial. He cried a bit, but as he looked to our right he nodded and smiled.

I asked "Why are you smiling?"

He said, "Tyler won't be in the box, it's just his body."

I was amazed to hear this wise spiritual information from a young child who hadn't been told about death, bodies, and spirits.

Since the funeral, there have been other times that Trevor has spoken about his brother playing with him. Once Trevor was playing with a truck in his sandbox. Afterward, he came into the house all dirty, with sand in his hair. He told me that Tyler had gotten dirty too and had to go to heaven to get cleaned up for nap time. I smiled because I hoped that he wasn't making this up. I cleaned him up and we talked a bit more about Tyler's passing. Trevor was holding my hand the entire time. As we went outside to tell Tyler night-night, a shower of stars fell over the house. I noticed that one very bright star was left behind right over our house. Trevor told me that Tyler had left it behind as a present. I smiled once more to help fight back the tears. How would a little three-year-old know enough to say that his baby brother left us a star as a gift, unless his brother was telling him this?

Trevor also reports that he talks to Tyler when we visit his gravesite. We take small trinkets and toys for Tyler to play with, and I have heard Trevor tell Tyler to pick them up when he gets done playing with them so that no one else will take them.

His last visit from Tyler was just a couple of days ago when he was sitting in the back of our truck. I heard him say, "Quit blowing spit!" I looked back at him, and he was leaning over as if propped up on some object and pointed his finger at something. He was grinning and blowing spit bubbles at whatever, or whomever, he was pointing at. When I asked what he was doing, he told me that Tyler did it first and that he was showing him the right way to blow the bubbles!

I'm a firm believer that my son has actually seen and heard from his baby brother. I know that he's not using these visits as an aid to help him get through grief, but they are innocent communications with his brother. I can only hope that they never end this amazing bond. These communications have given me an enormous amount of comfort, and I believe that's why God has allowed them.

My family has a history of the kids seeing apparitions. I have seen them growing up and still see them in my dreams. I also remember that when Trevor was younger, he would talk about seeing angels. He described them not as having wings but glowing brightly and watching him. Before Tyler passed, Trevor would walk around the house and outside as though he was holding someone's hand. When asked whom he was walking with, he would describe either my great-grandmother or his father's uncle—both of whom he had never met.

—*Jaime Stuckey*
www.findagrave.com

The Headless Barbie

My granddaughter Katie, since the young age of two years old, has been mentioning that my deceased daughter Kimberly (nicknamed "Sis") was in the room with her. Little Katie would smile and talk to someone whom no one else could see.

If we tried to humor her by saying something like, "Ha-ha-ha, you have a new friend," she would emphatically correct us by saying, "No, it's Sis!"

Katie was conceived three years after her Aunt Sis had passed, so she never knew Sis.

We would find Katie staring a lot at the orange round recliner couch, which was a favorite of Sis's. Sis had sat there especially during the last weeks before she passed at the age of nineteen from a form of cancer called Hodgkin's disease. Katie would also lie on that big orange couch and coo and smile and kick at the corner where Sis used to sit. Katie actually laughed out loud for the first time during one of these playful episodes.

Since having been to the Prayer Wave for After-Death Communication website, and learning, understanding, and experiencing personally afterlife contacts from my daughter Sis, I was aware babies and little children often see loved ones who have passed over. So I wasn't too surprised at Katie's behavior. Katie's mom, Nikki, was a little surprised though, even though she too has been visited quite a bit from her sister Sis.

Now for the big mindblower. One day when Katie was three years old, I heard her playing with her Barbie dolls in her bedroom. She was singing, praying, and talking in a lengthy, animated conversation to someone. Thinking nothing of it and thinking she is just a child playing with imaginary friends, I stopped in to give her a kiss. She said, "Nana, Sis is here."

I immediately got goose bumps and said, "Sis who?"

Katie replied, "My Sis, your baby; she is playing with me. She likes Barbies, but my mom [Nikki] used to pull the heads off hers."

I just stood there astonished, because Nikki really used to do that as a child. So I asked, "Katie, did your mom tell you about that?"

"No, Nana. Sis just did."

"Oh, Katie, who is Sis to you?"

"My voice, Nana."

I froze at that statement.

Katie then went on to say that if she was scared at night (which she often was), Sis would come to keep her company and pray with her, and it would be okay. She said Sis rides with us on the long rides to go see Grandpa at the rigs in Oklahoma. Katie said she loves Sis and Sis loves her. As Katie continued talking to me, she would intermittently declare, "And Sis says so," as if Sis were speaking directly through her to me. I was blown away once more.

Katie continues to make statements to me like, "No lie, Nana," and "I love Sis and John." (John is my son who passed when Katie was only a month old.)

Katie also talks about wanting to hug Jesus. I do not know what this is about. Just out of the blue, Katie will say at times, "Gosh, I want to hug Jesus."

"Honey, He loves you too."

"Yes, but I *need* to hug Him," Katie said.

She says this in a way that makes me feel she has hugged Jesus in the past. She also talks about Jesus as if He lives here with us.

I am so blessed to know my daughter Sis looks over her little niece from Heaven and has been helping to take away some of her night terrors. I also found out that she has been teaching Katie to understand good behavior from bad. I believe Sis still watches over her; just ask Katie.

I hope this is a story someone will find inspiring and helpful. Love and Blessings,

—*Mona Akin, Texas*

The Guys in My Room

My middle son, Mitchell, had an experience when he was four years old. He'd been having problems sleeping through the night, and one night around 2 A.M., he came into my room and asked if I'd please come see the "guys" who were in his room. I told him there were no guys in his room, and he was just seeing shadows. I reassured him that he was safe. However, he said he wasn't scared, but that there were four guys in his room, and he asked me to lie in his bed until they came back. I had lain down with him, and as I began to drift off to sleep, I heard him whisper, "Mom, do you see them? They're over in the corner. They're white. Who *are* they?"

I didn't see anything in any corners of the room and again assured him that we were alone. He insisted, "No, they're here. They're watching us, but they're good guys. I think one is Uncle Pat."

It was then that I knew who the men were. There are four men who I love dearly who are in heaven—my brother Pat who had been murdered, my best guy friend from high school, my grandfather, and the man I had fallen in love with whom I had planned to marry. I pray to all four of them every day, and I know that they were the guys watching over my son, Mitchell.

I told Mitch that we were lucky because we had some angels in the room with us and that they would keep him very safe. I told him that I'd stay with him because I wanted to be near the angels too. We began to fall asleep when he said, "Mom, did you feel that? He's by the bed. He touched me right on my back, and it feels soft like a chipmunk!" It was a great moment. I believe my son felt the touch of an angel that night from one of the guys.

I pray daily and I pray for signs a lot. I pray for the awareness to recognize them when they occur, as well as to be courageous enough to follow them.

—Erin Ryan, Pennsylvania

Grampy Joe

My mother-in-law stopped by one afternoon with a brown envelope containing photos. She sat down on a chair, and my daughter Kirsten, who was four years old at the time, climbed up on the chair to be close to her grandmother. As my mother-in-law was sliding an upside down 8 x 10 inch portrait out of the envelope, my daughter pointed her finger directly at the envelope and exclaimed, "That's Grampy Joe," as she giggled happily.

My mother-in-law looked at me in complete shock. I had no clue whether this was really Grampy Joe's photo because he had died about three years prior to my meeting my husband. Also, I had never seen any photos of him. I asked my mother-in-law whether this really was a picture of him, and she shook her head up and down.

My mother-in-law asked, "Kirsten, you know Grampy Joe?"

"Of course, Grandmom! He is so funny and he makes me laugh. Only he gets sad and cries sometimes because you don't know he is here, and he had to leave all of you behind," Kirsten said.

My mother-in-law then dropped the envelope to the floor looking as if she might faint. She took a minute to compose herself, then said, "My father was never a sissy of a man, but before he died, he cried like a baby because he had to leave all of us. He also had the most humorous personality of any man I knew. He would have a room full of people on the floor laughing with very little effort."

I knew my daughter has seen angels since she was able to tell me about them, so I was not too surprised. Still, I looked for some logical explanation as to how she could identify a man whom she had never met or had seen any photos of or even knew his name. It made no sense to me. So I called my husband, thinking perhaps he had shown a picture of his grandfather to her at some point, or maybe he had spoken about him to Kirsten, even mentioning his name. Something or anything that would make some sense of this.

My husband said the only pictures that even existed of his grandfather were those in his mother's attic in a box, which he hadn't seen in years. As far as mentioning Grampy Joe to Kirsten, since she was so young, he didn't see a reason to mention him or his name to her. So there was just no way that she would have known about him or that he was called Grampy Joe. Kirsten did not know what he looked like or what he was like personalitywise.

Even when Kirsten was ten years old, she still seemed to have some connection to him. For no reason, when the doorbell rang on its own and no one was there, she would say, "That is Grampy Joe!" Why this connection to him? We do not know. Maybe he is her guardian angel, maybe she can see things that we just cannot see, or maybe we are just not aware enough to notice.

—*Karen Janney, New Jersey*

The Electric Organ

Grandma was my best friend. When she was still here on this earth she would often joke and tell me, in a kidding and loving way, that she was going to haunt me when she was gone. She would say, "Well, I need to check up on you!" My dear, sweet grandma passed on August 13, 2003. Sadly, she missed my son Logan's birth by only two months. So they never met each other.

When she was still able-bodied, she immensely enjoyed playing her electric organ. She would often tell me that she wanted me to take her electric organ someday. After she passed, some time went by, and then my grandpa suggested that we take the organ home. My son Logan would always play with it when we were over at Grandpa's house, and Grandpa wanted him to enjoy playing it at home whenever he wanted to.

So at my grandpa's request we brought the organ home. Logan was only one and a half years old at the time and started playing on it the same day we brought it home. He just loved it. His little fingers were playing musical notes of happiness. My mother and I were standing to the right of Logan and were watching him happily playing on Grandma's electric organ. Suddenly Logan turned to the left, looked at the empty doorway and said, "Hi, Gamma!" Mind you, he never had the personal pleasure of knowing this wonderful woman who was his great-grandma. My mother and I looked at each other and started to cry a little. We had been constantly praying for a sign from Grandma since she passed, and those tiny words from a child, who was still open enough to see those loved ones who have passed, helped to deliver it that day.

—*Barbara Seeger*

Can't You See Her in Bed?

My mother passed away October 20,2001, from cancer. This was a devastating blow to our family. The morning that my mother passed away, she kept saying that she wanted to see or speak with someone. We were unsure as to whom she wanted to see or speak with, since she had already seen all her family. So my youngest sister, Mary Jo, put the telephone to our mother's ear and called her own house. The person on the other end speaking was Mary Jo's little three-year-old daughter, Brianna. When my mother heard Brianna's voice, she tried to speak with her. I knew then it was my niece Brianna who my mother wanted to see or hear one more time.

A few months after our mother had passed away, Mary Jo had Brianna by the hand leading her through their kitchen to go upstairs for a nap. Brianna suddenly stopped at the door in the kitchen. This door is the same one my mother and I would use to enter into their home. Brianna looked at the door and said to her mother, "Grandma Yooie is at the door. Why don't you let her in?" (This was the name that Brianna called her grandmother.)

Mary Jo was quite taken aback because Brianna didn't understand that her grandmother had passed away or what passing away actually meant. As they continued on their way upstairs, Brianna was adamantly asking why her mother wasn't letting her Grandma Yooie in the door!

While Brianna and my sister were lying in bed, Brianna started talking to someone.

Mary Jo asked, "Who are you talking to?"

"I'm talking to Grandma. Can't you see her in bed with us?"

As Brianna was finally falling off to sleep, she was hugging her pillow and told my sister Mary Jo that she was hugging her grandmother.

I feel this comforting visit was due to prayer as I had prayed and asked my mother for a sign. I also asked her to let us know that she was still with us and that there was life after death. My mother answered those burning questions that day by her appearance to Brianna.

—*Toni Jones, Pennsylvania*

When I Was Waiting to Be Born

My father passed away suddenly at fifty-three years young. He was an incredible human being who dearly loved children and was loved by them in return. He lived long enough to see my brother's first two children but never got to meet my husband or my two children, which bothers me to this day. The best description of who he was is on his tombstone, written by his then five-year-old grandson who insisted on "writing" on Poppy's tombstone:

Poppy was a kind man.
Poppy was a good man.
Poppy was a funny man.

One day I drove two hours down to Children's Hospital of Philadelphia with my two young children in the backseat. This was one of many trips for my son Matthew's numerous medical problems. On the way down, my three-year-old daughter Nicole was chatting away while I was talking to her. I can't remember exactly what we were talking about, but I think I was telling her not to take the straps of her car seat off and to sit there safely.

Suddenly I heard her say, "Don't worry, Murray."

I was taken aback by that particular expression, which I hadn't heard in years. I asked, "Do you know who used to say that?"

"Of course I know," she said, a bit exasperated at my stupidity. "Poppy!"

I was astonished and replied, "How did you know that, since you have never met Poppy?"

She very confidently said, "Yes I did. I used to speak to him all the time."

I said, "Nicole, Poppy was in heaven long before you were ever born."

"I know that, Mommy, that's where we used to talk when I was waiting to be born!"

Wow! Was I speechless! My dad had already met my daughter before I even did! This was extremely comforting to me.

—*Mary Beaury Paladino*

The Matt

When my granddaughter Breanna Lindahl was six months old, my son, who was her Uncle Matt, committed suicide. He was very close to his niece. In fact, just the day before he died, he and Breanna had their picture taken together; he was holding her and giving her a kiss good-bye before he left for work. Since Breanna was so young when Matt passed on, there was no way she could have remembered much of anything about him. We have taught her, and all of the grandkids, to pray nightly and to ask Matt to watch over them.

As soon as Breanna was old enough to talk, she would talk to Matthew's pictures. However, it began to strike me as strange when she was three years old and started to be afraid to go upstairs by herself. We would ask her why, and she would tell us that "the Matt" was up there. At first I thought she was saying "the man," that maybe she had a dream that scared her. But she looked at Matt's picture and said, "No, Grammy, I mean 'the Matt,' is the one up there."

Another time I was in the kitchen, washing dishes, crying my heart out as I was having "A Matt Day," and she came up to me, hugged me, and said, "Don't cry, Grammy, I will be your little buddy now." That was the name we always called Matt, but it would have been impossible for her to have remembered that on her own as she was only six months old when he passed.

Nowadays she loves to be alone upstairs, and there are times I hear her talking to her Uncle Matt; however, I do not interrupt. I feel this is her special time to share with him.

I know in my heart that my son talks to his niece daily, and it does enrich my life as I know he is safe and happy. Breanna tells me so.
—*Vicki Heckroth, Iowa*

Where Is Mom Mom's Blanket?

My very own granddaughter Judie Angelina has brought me heavenly words from my mother. Since the time Judie Angelina was born, she would stare at a corner of the room, near where we all would sit to watch TV. I never knew what she was staring at until one day she started to smile at that same wall. Then she started to laugh. I felt very strongly that she was seeing one of my deceased parents who was causing her to laugh. We all believed that this little baby had a special gift from God.

When Judie Angelina was two and a half years old something un-explainable happened. I had a unique quilt that I had made from my mother's clothes after she passed. This quilt is very dear to me. I had it in a box under my bed because we had just moved, and I wasn't sure where I wanted to store it permanently. Judie Angelina was not aware of this quilt, nor did she know that it was stored under my bed. However, one day I was sitting on my bed with Judie Angelina, and we were playing with her blanket. I had it sitting on top of my head. For some reason I asked her, "Where is Mom Mom's blanket?" Mom Mom was the name that my children called my mother. I thought Judie Angelina was going to point to the blanket, but in-stead that little baby girl got down off the bed, looked under the bed, and pointed to the box. I was shocked! I took the box out. Then Judie Angelina opened it on her own and pointed to the quilt. Now she had never ever seen that quilt! Well, I looked at her in sheer and utter amazement. I then just started to cry and hugged my little baby granddaughter. I just knew that my mother was in the room with us and that she had told Judie Angelina exactly where her quilt was.

Judie Angelina is older and a lot of things have happened in indi-cating that my mother talks to her. One day when she was in the tub, she told me that she felt Mom Mom's hand on her shoulder. She told me that she could only see her hand and a little bit of her arm. She also said that Mom Mom never wore nail polish while she was with us on earth, but she has it on now and it was pink!

My mom's favorite color was pink, and it is true that my mom never wore nail polish. You see, the reason is that she worked in a factory for forty-five years. She made valves for ships and worked with her hands, which caused her hands to be continually rough and sore, so she didn't wear rings or nail polish. Once again I knew my mom was communicating through my grandbaby, giving her this validating information for me to hear.

My grandbaby knows things about my mom that have astounded

me. She was born after my mother passed over, so no one will ever convince me that she didn't meet her in Heaven or that she doesn't communicate with her now on earth. Because of Judie Angelina, I feel like my mom is always here with us!

I am so blessed by God, and I am happy to find out that my grandbaby has this spiritual gift. If I can help one person believe and understand what the afterlife holds, and in fact that there is an afterlife, it would mean the world to me!

—*Judie Ziegler Alliano, New Jersey*

Bowling with Tony

My twenty-one-year-old son Tony was killed in an automobile accident, along with his cousin Justin and Justin's future sister-in-law in December 2004. Tony and Justin were very accomplished bowlers. They both started to bowl at the very young age of four, and they had both achieved perfect three hundred games before their early deaths.

Two and a half years later after they had passed on, I was sitting on the porch watching my two-year-old granddaughter Jayden playing. (My granddaughter Jayden had not yet been born at the time of this devastating tragedy.) One day while I was watching her play, I noticed that she was rolling a rock down the sidewalk. I asked her what she was doing, and she said she was bowling with Tony. Now Jayden had never been bowling, and as I mentioned, her Uncle Tony had passed over before she was born.

I did a double take and said excitedly, "What did you say?"

"I'm bowling with Tony. See him?" Jayden said.

"I can't see him," I said.

"He is right *there*!" she said.

"Where?" hoping to get a glimpse of my son again.

At this, Jayden got very frustrated with me, so she bent down and pointed to the ground and said, "Tony is right *there*! Do you see him?"

I didn't see him, but I have no doubt that Jayden was bowling with her Uncle Tony that day, and this was very comforting for me to know.

—*Debby Schaaf*

Apple Davey

One night at the dinner table, my then three-year-old little boy Logan had just come in from playing in the sandbox outside. He was walking along and singing the words, "Apple Davey, Apple Davey."

"What are you singing?" I asked.

"Apple Davey!"

"Who's that?"

"He's Davey. He's a girl. He's dead. He died on the road."

My eyes almost popped out of my head when my son said that. I immediately thought of my boyfriend Dave who had passed in 1990. Dave was a musician and he had very long hair. He passed in a drinking-and-driving-related accident, and he did die on the road. I knew my little boy had never seen a guy with long hair, so he might very well refer to Dave by saying, "He's a girl." This was amazing and comforting to me.

—*Barbara Seeger*

Little Poppy

After the death of my father-in-law, we moved into his house. My middle child, who was between three and four years old at the time, often played in the living room with her toys. One day I was in the kitchen from where I could partially see into the living room where she was playing. I could hear her talking and moving about. She was a late bloomer talking, so when words came out that we could understand, I often would take special note of it and would really listen to her.

She'd been playing for a while when I heard her giggling and saying, "I see you!" She did this a few more times before I asked her what she was doing. She giggled and said she was playing with "Little Poppy." She was using my father-in-law's nickname that my other kids used to call him, although it didn't initially register with me who Little Poppy was.

I walked to the doorway of the living room to get a better view of what was going on. She was standing in the middle of the room looking up at the far left corner of the ceiling and pointing up at that spot. She giggled again and asked if I could see the pretty light. When I looked in the corner, I didn't see anything. She giggled again and told me that it was Little Poppy. I realized that she was referring to my father-in-law, so I gently reminded her that Little Poppy was dead, but she continued to insist that he was up in that corner.

Something distracted my attention, and I walked away for a minute. When I came back to her, she told me that he was bye-bye. We found her doing this a few more times, but every time we would enter the room she was playing in, she would tell us he had gone bye-bye.

—*Pamela, Pennsylvania*

Don't Let the Bedbugs Bite

My grandmother died when I was sixteen years old. She raised me from the time I was a baby. In essence, she was my mother. Her death hit me very hard. I became closed off to the world and rebelled by running off.

When I was twenty, I gave birth to my little daughter, Ashley. By now I was living with my aunt on the same land where I grew up with my grandmother. Even though they renovated the house, I could still feel Granny's presence there. The room I was staying in used to be the living room where Granny would always sit after she was finished with her chores.

Granny has visited my daughter Ashley several times over the years. Once when Ashley was four years old, Granny woke her up when she was having a bad dream. Ashley said she saw a lady by her bed who told her to wake up and said that it was okay and that she would keep her safe. I showed Ashley a picture of Granny, and her eyes got real wide, and she said, "That's her, Momma! That's her!"

I explained, "She was your great-grandmother, and she will always protect you."

My granny has also come to see my other daughter Cheyenne, and I believe she protected her through my entire pregnancy. One morning, when Cheyenne was almost four years old, she came into my bedroom and said that when she went to sleep the night before, she felt someone tucking the covers around her, and she thought it was me. She opened her eyes and saw a lady smiling at her and the lady said, "Sleep tight and don't let the bedbugs bite."

I started to cry because I knew it was Granny right off. She used to tuck my sister and me into bed the same way saying, "Sleep tight and don't let the bedbugs bite."

I know my kids will always have their granny as their guardian angel. My heart still hurts because she is physically gone, but it helps that I know she comes and visits. When I look into Cheyenne's eyes, I see my granny looking back at me; Cheyenne has her same eyes. That is very comforting.

God Bless you all.

—*Georgina Warren, Texas*
www.myspace.com/whispix

The Broken Dryer

On July 19, 2006, the saddest news hit our family. My sister Maria's boyfriend, Terrance, had passed over very unexpectedly. Terrance had recently turned thirty-two. He was a very healthy person with a very wholesome lifestyle. He came into my sister's life a year earlier.

We believed he came into her life after her sad marriage and divorce to show her finally the true meaning of love. Maria glowed from Terrance's love.

Terrance was from Washington, DC, and we lived in New York, so our family did not have the chance to meet him personally. Through pictures and letters and through my sister's telling us all about him, we felt we knew him well. Terrance was fond of my son Anthony who was three years old at the time Maria and Terrance met. Maria would tell or write to Terrance about how fast Anthony was growing and how articulate Anthony was for a three-year-old. Even though Terrance never met Anthony personally, he would tell Maria that he believed someday Anthony would be a football or basketball player.

On July 15, 2006, Terrance was admitted to the hospital because for the past year he had been passing out at his basketball games, and the doctors were unable to determine what was causing this to happen. Four days later, he was operated on and Terrance died while in the recovery room. This was devastating to my sister Maria who loved him so very much.

Twelve days after Maria came back from the funeral, she came over to visit us and was talking about Terrance. During this conversation my son Anthony, who had turned four years old, used a little fresh five-letter word beginning with "*b*". Maria told him that Terrance didn't like those kinds of words, and Anthony apologized.

We went to bed around 1:00 A.M. A short time later, Anthony woke me up because he had to go to the bathroom. As we were walking down the stairs, Anthony waved and said, "Hello, Terrance!"

"Who are you talking to?" I asked.

"Terrance. He's in the kitchen. Mommy, are you going to talk to Terrance?"

"Anthony, Terrance is *not* in the kitchen."

"Oh yes he is, and he is mad at me." Anthony crossed his arms and made a face!

I asked, "Oh yeah, if he is there, what color are the clothes he's wearing?"

"Blue and white."

It shocked me to hear those colors because Terrance had been buried in a dark blue suit with a white shirt.

A few days later, I was at the Laundromat, and there was a Broken Dryer sign on one of the machines. Anthony saw the same sign but saw a different message. He said to me that the sign was a note to Terrance from Aunt Maria saying, "Terrance, I miss you a lot. See you in Heaven. Love you always, Maria."

I later told my sister about the words on the sign that only Anthony saw in the Laundromat. She was shocked. She said that she had placed a number of cards and letters in Terrance's casket, but there was one note she wrote that read exactly like Anthony had seen on the Broken Dryer sign!

Another time Anthony mentioned that he saw Terrance in the trees with the squirrels and the nuts. I told my sister about this sighting. Again, she was shocked because squirrels and nuts had been a private joke between Terrance and Maria.

I have also received personal messages from Terrance. However, the things that only Maria would know about came through my child. I believe their love was beautiful, and now that he is gone, Anthony is Terrance's little messenger to help comfort and strengthen my sister.

—*Miriam Pereyra, New York*

Who Was Ash-a-lee?

My husband's grandparents used to sleep in the bedroom where my youngest child Michelle now sleeps. One day when Michelle was about three years old, she was playing happily in her bedroom. Then she came downstairs and came bouncing into the kitchen telling me her *best* friend Ashley wants a drink. Knowing that there was no one in the house at the time except the two of us, I told her that only one juice cup at a time can be used upstairs.

Now my daughter had a speech problem, so for me to understand what she was actually saying was always quite a task. But every time she mentioned her best friend, it was very clear and understandable. It usually sounded like Ash-a-lee. She would often tell anyone who would listen to her, that her best friend Ash-a-lee was doing this or that with her. This went on for about a year. Eventually Michelle started to attend half-day prekindergarten, so other things seemed to take over her attention and Ash-a-lee slipped away.

When Michelle was nearly six years old, she remembered once again about playing with Ash-a-lee when she was younger. Michelle explained to us that Ash-a-lee was a child who was a little older than she was at the time. We did research into both sides of our families but could not find an Ashley.

Something else peculiar, but yet helpful, used to happen when Michelle was still sleeping in her crib. She was a sundial sleeper (a child who starts out lying in one position and throughout the night rotates around like a sundial). Her bedding and toys would end up in chaos. Most of the time, the toys would be on the floor.

My husband or I would check on her before we would go to bed. Exhausted, many nights I would go into her room to straighten it up, only to discover that she was all covered up, and all her toys would be back in her crib and neatly tidied up! I would thank my husband for doing this for me, only to have him tell me he had forgotten to check on her or that he thought I had already done so! Could the help have come from Ash-a-lee or my husband's grandfather who used to sleep in that bedroom before he passed in that very room? Being an exhausted mom, I really appreciated the help that I was getting, wherever it was coming from!

—*Pamela, Pennsylvania*

Guess Who's Here?

Christopher is my son who tragically ended his own life on May 30, 2005. My daughter's son Zachary was only seven months old when he saw him last. My mother, who is Zach's great-grandma, passed over just eight days after my son Chris. So we had back-to-back significant losses in our family.

When my grandson Zachary was two years old, my daughter Sheena was getting him ready for bed at night when all of a sudden he turned to her and asked, "Mommy, guess who's here?"

"I don't know, honey, who is here?"

"Chris and Grandma!"

My daughter Sheena got a little freaked realizing Zachary was referring to her deceased brother and Zachary's great-grandma. She managed to appear calm in front of Zachary and asked him some questions, but he just ignored her. This was the first encounter Zachary had with spirits—that we know of.

The second encounter with spirits was when Zach was two and a half years old, and I, his grandmother, was staying over one night. I work nights, so I got to Sheena's place around 4:30 A.M. and slept in the second bedroom. Zachary didn't know I was there.

My bedroom door was closed. Zachary's bedroom was right across the hall, and his door was closed too. I awoke to hear Zachary talking to someone. I could hear him very well. He was talking very clearly and loudly about his animals and his toys. I could hear him saying, "And, Grandma, this is my bear, and this is my truck, and this is my dinosaur." I wasn't sure to *whom* he was talking, so I snuck out my door and went over to his room and just listened through the closed door. Then I heard Zachary say, "Grandma, where you go? Where are you at?" I immediately *knew* he was being visited by my mom, who is his great-grandma.

I waited for a few seconds before I opened the door, and when he saw me, he smiled and said, "Hi Bama." (Zachary, from day one since he could talk, has always called me Bama—never Grandma.)

"What are you doing?" I asked.

"Playing," he said.

"Is Grandma visiting today?" I asked.

Of course he ignored me, so I dropped the subject. I believe Zachary is being "visited" by our loved ones quite often.

My daughter Sheena has mentioned to me a number of times that Zachary would giggle out loud for no reason or would look out from their porch and smile and point at someone or something when no one was there.

When Zachary would come over to my house, he would pick up a picture I have of my son Chris and would just look at it, or he would stroke it and sometimes just carry it around with him. I firmly believe that Zachary has been able to see and talk to my son Chris and my mother since they have passed.

We, as a family, have gotten very spiritual since my son's death. We have learned a lot more about the afterlife. I also believe that prayer has a lot to do with our beliefs and our spirituality. We miss the physical presence of our loved ones, and that will never change, but just knowing that they are in Heaven gives peace and joy to our hearts and brings smiles to our faces. It truly sets our minds at ease knowing that death is not an ending, but a beginning to a new life. Realizing that our loved ones are happy puts our minds at ease. We know they are around us watching out for the little ones and us, and for that we are grateful.

—*Nancy Hachmann*

Payless Shoes

My daughter Stormy was born in 1996. She was two years old when my dad died in 1998. She was with him every day except the day that he died. A whole year had gone by before she ever mentioned her "papaw," and when she did, it was because of a specific request she said he made.

Stormy and I were driving through a parking lot of a shopping center when she suddenly said to me, "Momma, let's go to Payless and get me some shoes!"

I did a double take and asked, "Do what?"

"Papaw said for you to take me and get me some new shoes!"

This was a very strange request for a few reasons: we had never shopped at Payless shoes before, she was not familiar with the store, she was only three years old, and she was not old enough to read the Payless shoe sign in the parking lot. It totally blew my mind that she would say this to me. I was so taken aback by this highly unusual request that I decided to go along with it. We went into Payless to browse around for some shoes. She picked out a pair of shoes she liked, and she said, "I think Papaw would like these."

Daily prayer is important in our household. I think maybe my daughter was thinking about her papaw, and I know kids are closer to God than we are, so who knows what went on that day between my child and my daddy.

—*Amy Washington, Texas*

Roller-Skating

One day my then two-and-a-half-year-old great-niece Lynnzee was sitting in the back of the family car in her car seat while her mother was driving. A song came on the radio that reminded her mother of an earlier time when she was a teenager roller-skating with her friends at a skating rink. Her mother only thought this and did not verbally express her memories out loud. While she was reminiscing about this pleasant past memory at the skating rink, Lynnzee said, "Mommy, I like to roller-skate too."

Her mother was stunned! How could Lynnzee possibly have known what her mother was thinking?

Lynnzee also claims to see a lady in the house that my nephew and

his wife are renting from his grandparents. When her mother is changing her in her bedroom she sometimes says, "Mommy, there's lady."

Nobody seems to know who she is. Lynnzee's great-grandmother
thinks it may be her late older sister who lived in that house with her
husband right before she died.

—*Daria, Connecticut*

He Has to Go Bye-Bye

In 2002 my husband and I adopted our daughter Noralee from
China. She was the light of my younger brother Tyler's life. Tyler and
I were very close, almost like twins, even though we were five years
apart in age. He loved children but was unable to have any of his
own, so my child was like his own too. He would come to my house
every day to help me with Noralee. They laughed and played and
seemed to have their own special bond.

In April 2004 we adopted our son Christian from Korea. Tyler
was overjoyed for us; now he had another baby to spoil! Sadly, one
month later Tyler was shot and killed. I was devastated. I could
barely function. Over and over I would pray, "Please, God, help
me." They were the only words I could manage to get out. God
knew my pain and my prayers did not need more words.

We hadn't told our then two-year-old daughter, Noralee, about
her Uncle Tyler as we were trying to absorb it all ourselves. We
weren't sure just how to explain it to her, so we held off doing so.
About a week after his death, Noralee said Uncle Tyler had come to
see her last night when she was sleeping on the couch. I started asking her a million questions. Noralee became exasperated with all my
questions. So she took me by the hand and said, "I was *here*, and I
opened my eyes and Uncle Tyler was *there*," pointing to the opposite
end of the couch. "He said he has to go bye-bye with his friend."

"Who was his friend?" I asked.

"I don't know."

"Was it a boy or a girl?"

"It was a boy, and he had to go bye-bye with his friend."

When she repeated this, she said it louder as she was annoyed that I couldn't understand something so simple.

I still don't know who was with Tyler, but I think it may have been my dad who died in 1978. I asked her if Uncle Tyler had said anything else to her, and she said, "He told me to be nice to Christian."

This gave me great comfort that Tyler had come to her and told her that he had to leave. She has never had any problems with his death. I believe she has accepted it because her Uncle Tyler came to her and explained he had to go.

—Toby Richard, Ohio

The Man in the Wall

When my daughter Jamie was three years old, she came and told me that she saw a "man in the wall." On a second occasion, she reported that she saw him again, but this time with a baby in his arms. I wasn't sure what this all meant or who the man could possibly be, so I never pursued it any further. Later the gentleman from whom we bought our property came over for a visit. He showed us a photo of his son and his family who once lived on our land. Jamie looked at the photo and declared that *he* was the man she had seen in the wall!

At first I didn't understand how Jamie could've seen the former owner's son in our wall, but the owner did. He explained that his son once had a house on this property, but it caught on fire and burned to the ground, killing his son and granddaughter. We were amazed at this.

—Teri Powell

Uncle Tony Was Watching You

In November 2004 my Uncle Tony passed away after a long battle with cancer. It is difficult for words to express how much he meant to my family and me. He was much more than an uncle. He was a second father to all of us. Whenever we needed Uncle Tony or his wife, my Aunt Elena, they were always right there.

I have two little girls, and my Uncle Tony loved them just as deeply as they loved him. My daughters Lia and Erica were just four and five years old, respectively, when he passed away.

After he died, my aunt gave me a framed picture of him, which I placed on a lamp table in our family room. I have a habit of watching TV and then falling asleep on the sofa in the family room. One night I fell asleep as usual on the sofa. My husband John did not want to disturb me, so he let me sleep, and he went upstairs to bed.

I suddenly awoke at 3 A.M. I sat up on the sofa and looked around the room because I had a very strong feeling and sense that my Uncle Tony was there with me. I smiled to myself and looked over at his picture and said, "Hi, Uncle Tony." It is difficult to explain, but I knew he was there with me, even though I couldn't see him. I then turned off the lights, made my way upstairs to my bedroom, and went to bed.

The next day, my daughter Lia, who was four years old, said, "Mommy, I had a dream about Uncle Tony last night."

I went over to her and gave her a hug as I put her on my lap. "What was the dream about?" I asked.

Lia looked at me smiling and said, "Mommy, I dreamed that you were sleeping on the sofa downstairs and Uncle Tony was watching you. When you woke up, he followed you upstairs."

What she said shocked me, but did not surprise me. I was shocked because what I had sensed the night before had actually been real. Yet, I was not totally surprised because I had a knowingness that my Uncle Tony had been there with me.

As I looked at her, I couldn't help but cry. My uncle was still with us and wanted us to know that he was. That meant the world to me.

—*Josie Varga, New Jersey*
Author, Visits from Heaven
www.josievarga.com

The Clown's Prayer

My brother Pat died in March 1995 after a brave battle with AIDS. He contracted it through a tainted blood transfusion he received in 1984 after being severely injured in a car accident.

His injuries from this accident were so extensive that the doctors were amazed that he had even survived. He had many broken bones (both legs, pelvis, shoulder, arm, etc.), a lacerated liver, and a punctured lung. Through the wonderful care he received from the many doctors and nurses and through his bravery and determination, Pat not only survived numerous surgeries and the eventual loss of his right lung, but he completely recuperated and moved on with his life.

Though Pat did not know he had received tainted blood at the time, he intuitively did feel that he was on borrowed time, and he stopped to "smell the roses," as they say. He met a wonderful woman named Denise and got married. Unfortunately, five years after his accident, he received a call from the Red Cross informing him that he had received infected blood and needed to be tested. Those follow-up tests showed that Pat had in fact contracted AIDS.

Through a lot of prayer and spiritual strength, he came to accept his illness; after all, he should have died in the car accident. Ironically the blood that saved his life was now killing him. He felt God had a purpose in keeping him around for a little while longer, and he decided he would use his time to reach out to others and help wherever he could. He spoke to teens about safe sex and drug addiction.

He also tried to spread the word that AIDS victims were just that—victims.

During this time our family pulled together and spent as many happy times with each other as we could. Pat especially reached out to his nieces and nephews. He wanted them to remember him as a happy, goofy, and generous uncle. It was very important to him that they remembered him, so he set about spending special times with them and giving them special gifts that he made such as paintings, poems, and prayers. He made sure he gave everyone a hand-painted copy of "The Clown's Prayer," which is a prayer about spreading more laughter and smiles than tears. The "Clown's Prayer" was a prayer given to Pat to signify how he spent his last years on earth. This was so true.

Each niece and nephew truly felt special to Uncle Pat, and that was his goal. The youngest of this bunch was my daughter Bridget who was almost a year old. For Christmas Pat and his wife Denise gave Bridget a baby-sized Irish Claddagh ring. The next month, on January 10, Bridget had her first birthday party. We held her birthday party at Pat's home because he was too sick to travel. As sick as Pat was, right before her party, he conned my brother Jim into taking him shopping. He bought Bridget an adult-sized Claddagh ring with her birthstone in it so that when she became an adult, she would have something to remember him by. But even after giving her a wonderful first birthday party and gift, Pat was sad because he was worried that she would forget about him. I promised that this would never happen, but still it bothered him a lot. Pat died just three months later. We were sad, but happy that his suffering had finally ended and that he was in the arms of God.

One year later, around Bridget's second birthday, on a day when all my other children were in school, I heard Bridget laughing and singing in the other room. She was having such a good time that I had to ask her what she was up to. She said she and Uncle Pat were playing a game, and he was making her laugh with his silly faces and a silly dance. I tried not to show how shocked I was, as I hid my tears. She was so happy and nonchalant about it all that I felt I shouldn't make a big deal out of it by questioning her any further.

A few days later, the same thing happened and soon it became a common occurrence. She would later share some funny story about Uncle Pat with us, and we all knew it was true, even with her limited vocabulary at two years old. No doubt, she was playing with her Uncle Pat.

One day the laughter stopped, and I heard her crying. She was inconsolable. I ran to her and asked what was wrong? She said Uncle Pat had to go and be with the angels. He told her he loved her and never to forget that. He also told her that he was going to visit her cousins for a while and that he would visit again, but not as often because he needed to be with the angels.

When Bridget was twelve she no longer remembered this particular good-bye story, but she remembered her Uncle Pat and the many times he played with her after he passed. She remembers how funny he was when he did his silly dance and made funny faces.

—*Bernadette Coffey*

Nona Helps to Take Her Shoes Off

My daughter Allie's grandparents, my husband's parents, passed over long before her birth, and it's always bothered me that she didn't have the chance to know them. They were wonderful people.

When Allie was an infant, I had to take quick showers while she was taking a nap in her crib, and I always asked my deceased mother-in-law to watch her while I was taking a shower. I always felt her presence and was comforted by it. I just knew Allie would be safe.

I started noticing that when Allie was two years old, she would be talking a lot while she was playing. Curious, I started listening in on her conversations. She was having conversations with her grandparents and referring to them as Papa and Nona while she was playing. After Allie saw a picture of them, she told me that Nona always helped her take her shoes off.

Allie is six years old now, and I still hear her talking to them, but not as often as when she was younger. I hope she never loses that connection, or at least, she will always remember those special play dates and Nona helping her take her shoes off. My husband and I are happy that his parents get to see Allie and still get to be around her, even though they have passed over.

—Jackie Cresci

Grandma Rayburn's Grave

My great-grandmother passed away when I was one month old. We never talked about my great-grandmother ever. One day my four-year-old daughter came to me and said, "Mommy, who is Grandma Rayburn?"

I replied, "She was my great-grandma. Why?"

She looked at me and said, "Oh, just wondered."

So I went about my business not giving it too much thought.

Later I was talking to my mom on the phone and asked her if she ever mentioned my great-grandmother to my daughter. She said, "No, why would you ask?"

So I went on to tell her about what had happened. It seems we both thought it was strange but didn't say anything more about it.

Then on Memorial Day my mom wanted to go to my great-grandma's grave, which is about an hour's drive from our house. Most of her family is buried there, so we were going to make a day of it. My dad, mom, husband, son, and daughter were all along for the ride. My mom was having a very difficult time remembering where they were all buried. So my husband dropped us off so that we could walk around and look for their gravesites. All of a sudden my daughter yelled, "Here it is! Here is Grandma Rayburn!"

I thought no way. How did she know that? We had never been there with her before, and not only was she just four years old, but she could not read yet. I about lost it because I realized that my Grandma Rayburn must have shown her the location of the grave.

My mom looked at me, and I looked at her and said, "See Mom, she *is* talking to her." I had heard that little ones could see and talk to the dead, but never believed it, until this!

The funny thing is, now if you were to ask my daughter about Grandma Rayburn, she would say, "Who is that?" She doesn't remember any of it.

I told her the story when she was sixteen, and she said, "Stop, Mom, you are creeping me out!" So I do believe in children connecting with our loved ones that have passed.

—*Shawnda Duffy, Ohio*

Hey, What Are You Doing Up There?

Connections to our loved ones, who have gone on before us, can come in all shapes and sizes and in simple, everyday occurrences. One of mine happened to come in the special form of a delightful little girl with brown curly hair named Haley. She is my adored niece, also my godchild, and being in her presence always brings a joyful smile to my face!

Haley came into the world in the fall of 1997, and our family began to realize early on that she was equipped with a wealth of insightful information and inquisitiveness expressed through her beautiful, deeply engaging, brown eyes. "An old soul" is what we proclaimed her to be to one another in agreement. Haley is observant and full of fun with a curious sense of wonder and speaks exactly what's on her mind!

Haley was almost two years old when her oldest cousin, my beloved son Jason, died in the summer of 1999 at the tender age of twenty-four. Jason was adored by his sister Jessica and each of his four younger cousins, Kyle, Rachel, Carlie D., and Haley, and his love for all of them was mutual. As a mother, I was grief stricken in the beginning stages of the profound loss of my firstborn child. I slowly began to find my way through the magnified darkness when acceptance, peace, and my strong faith in God started to console me. One day in November during that initial period of time when such unexpected mourning was incomprehensible, little Haley, in all her purity and innocence, instinctively helped me realize her cousin Jason's spirit continued to participate in our lives and watched over us as a guardian angel.

As my son's twenty-fifth birthday on the twenty-second of November was approaching without him, it was turning out to be a somber, heart-wrenching period. How does a mother celebrate the initial birthday of her precious child without his physical presence? It was excruciating anticipating that upcoming day.

One cold and windy day during that dreaded month of November, Haley; her mother, Luanne, who is my younger sister; Haley's older sister, Rachel; and I visited the gravesite of their baby sister, Diana. (Baby Diana was delivered to my Luanne and her husband prematurely and lived only a few hours. Diana's brief stay in our family was a defining moment and paved the way for more sadness to come in a year's time.)

Returning to my house for lunch after paying our respects to baby Diana, I made Haley a peanut butter and jelly sandwich, a special request of hers. As I turned toward Haley with her luncheon plate, I noticed that she was intently gazing at the corner of my kitchen ceiling by the basement door where my son Jason had often descended in life to play pool and occasional card games with family and friends.

Suddenly and unexpectedly, Haley blurted out, "Hey! What are you doing up there?" I turned to look in her focused direction, and upon seeing nothing, I excitedly asked whom she saw. In a split second, without answering, Haley became preoccupied with her sandwich, licking jelly off the bread! I didn't press for answers because Haley was a toddler. However, my hunch was that she saw the spiritual energy of my son in a form only she could recognize with those soulful eyes.

Then as further validation in 2008, I was taking care of my greatniece Isabelle, who was two years old at the time. She and I were standing by the cellar door where Haley had nine years earlier looked up at the ceiling as a toddler and said, "Hey! What are you doing up there?"

I was stooped down in front of Isabelle talking to her, and I could see she was intently looking over my head. Curious, I asked her what she was looking at. She told me that she was looking at "the big guy." Well my son Jason stood six feet two inches tall. I asked Isabelle if it was Jason (same as I did with Haley) but never got an answer. I believe it was the spirit of Jason that Isabelle saw, just like Haley!

It was exhilarating to have validation of the presence of Jason's spirit from these children of God and to sense the true potential that our spirits do indeed survive death and stay connected to family. This glimmer of hope created an unforgettable impression I will hold dear to my heart for the rest of my life! It was a gift of faith, which unfolded before me, reinforcing intuitive feelings I cling to that my son's spirit is very much alive and happy on the other side of God's magnificent rainbow.

I believe the angelic message through Haley that day in November 1999 and from Isabelle nine years later were offerings from my beloved son of proof of his continued existence and his eternal love. With God's guidance, Jason was allowed to present his spiritual aura during his birthday month through the translucent vision and sweetest announcement by this beautiful child named Haley and again through sweet Isabelle.

—Helen, Massachusetts

You Didn't Touch My Lips

My mom passed on August 8, 2003, while I was pregnant with my son. I was the one who found her, and I started to pray for signs from her from that time on.

About three years later, my four-year-old daughter Alexandria gave me two indications that my mother was with us. The first was when I gave my daughter a kiss good-night, and she said, "You didn't touch my lips!" (When I was a child my mother and grandpa used to say that to us in order to get another kiss.)

"Where did you hear that?"

"Nana."

Then a few days later, we were driving in the car and she said, "Mom, you are supposed to tell us, there is no laughing allowed in the house."

Because that was one of my dad's sayings, I asked, "Did Grandpa tell you to tell me that?"

"No, Nana told me to tell you."

I almost cried both times. It was amazing and joyful to learn this. Since then I have asked my daughter if she still sees Nana, and she told me, yes, that Nana tells her funny stories. I don't doubt it.

—*Margarite Fisher, Illinois*

See Mom Dancing?

Mom had not been in good health for many years and had lost all but a small portion of her kidney. She felt miserable most of the time. Still, she had a great mind and a quick sense of humor.

While my mom was still alive, my little four-year-old grand-daughter Katie heard us all refer to my mother as Mom. Katie began calling her Mom too, not Grandmother or Mona Lisa like some of my children did, but Mom. She liked to talk to Mom and liked to try to help her as much as a four-year-old could. Even though my mother was not always in the mood to have children around her, she and Katie bonded anyway.

My mom had a major heart attack and entered hospice in December 2006. She was only there for four days before she passed away. We complied with her wishes and took her body back to our hometown of Dumas where my dad was buried. She was laid to rest beside him after twenty-three years of greatly missing him.

When my mom passed, we had the honor of driving the priest from here in Wichita Falls, Texas, to preside over her service in Dumas, Texas. Father K. had been a friend of my mother's for eighteen years. The first time Father K. visited her, Mom had asked him to officiate at her funeral if he outlived her. He promised he would, and he did. Father rode with Katie and me for the five-hour drive to Dumas. Father thought Katie was so gifted and spiritual for such a young lady.

At the viewing service, when it was time for the rosary to be said, Father K. asked me to make sure that Katie really wanted to go up to the coffin to see the body. I did my best to explain that Mom was now in Heaven with my other children, her Aunt Sissy and Uncle John, and that this was just Mom's body there. We were here just to say good-bye.

Katie really wanted to go up to the coffin, so she walked down to the front and knelt down in front of it. She said something to my mother that we could not hear. Then she stood back up and took Father K's hand and said, "Be very quiet. Mom is asleep."

The next day when we were driving back to Wichita Falls after the funeral with Father K. and Katie in the car, Katie said, "Nana, look at the sky; it's beautiful."

There was a nice Texas sunset, but nothing unusual. I said, "Yes it is."

Katie pointed to the sky and said, "See Mom dancing with that man in black pants, who I don't know? She is in a beautiful red dress and they are happy."

My dad was buried in dark pants and a sweater, so I believed in my heart that Katie saw my mom dancing with my dad. Katie never knew my dad, her great-grandfather, as he had passed long before Katie was born.

I looked at Father K. He just smiled at me and said, "I wish we could see what God lets the little children see."

I feel that my mom wanted me to know through Katie that she is now happy and with my dad after twenty-three years of waiting to be reunited with him. Katie continues to talk some days about Mom, but never with sadness.

—*Mona Akin, Texas*

JJ Likes to Take a Bath Too

I lost my son Justin to a motorcycle accident a year ago. He was only twenty years old. A few months later my two-and-a-half-year-old daughter was taking a bath, and I noticed that she started to whisper to someone for a few minutes. So I asked her, "Who are you whispering to?"

"JJ." (She always called her brother JJ.)

"What are you whispering about?"

"JJ told me that he likes to take a bath too, and he wishes he could play with me right now, and then he said he loves me."

I cried when she told me about their sweet conversation.

There have been other times when she said JJ spoke to her. He has told her that she was pretty in her princess dress as well as telling her other small things. I love to hear about these conversations. I just smile and tell her that it was wonderful that she and JJ talk to each other and that it makes me very happy.

—*Raelene Cardone-Akgul*
www.myspace.com/justin_cutright

He's Funny

Ashley Anne Marie Baucom is my youngest granddaughter. She is the daughter of my son Ashley, who died at the young age of twenty-three. His daughter was born four months after he died.

When Ashley Anne was less than two years old, I started to notice that she would look up and laugh and giggle when sitting or lying down. She would also sit and play games with *someone* unseen. I often wondered what was going on, but chalked it up to the usual childhood imaginary friends explanation.

Because my son Ashley's spirit had visited me on several occasions after he passed, the thought came to mind that perhaps she was seeing her daddy. So one day when Ashley Anne was almost three years old, I asked her, "Who are you playing with?"

She walked over to her daddy's photo and said, "I play with my daddy when he comes. He makes me laugh a lot. He told me that he loves me very much, and I told him that I loved him back very much. He's funny."

My son was known as the family comic. This child had never known, nor had she ever seen her daddy when he was alive on earth. Yet to this very day, two years later, she still talks of how he visits her every once in a while. Even now Ashley Anne says that she will see her daddy again when she goes to Heaven and that I will see him too. My son Ashley also told her how much he loves me.

It is good to know that Ashley not only lives on in his daughter but also lives on in Heaven and visits his beloved ones on earth.

—*Donna Bowman, Florida*
Author, The Walking Wounded
thewalkingwoundedauthordonnabowman.blogspot.com

Balloons and Christmas Presents

My twenty-year-old son Justin, my nephew, and my son's future sister-in-law were all killed in an automobile accident in December 2004. My son left us a beautiful grandson named Colton. The following is just one of the times my grandson Colton spoke of a communication with his deceased daddy.

Colton was two years old at the time of this occurrence. I brought Colton to a restaurant to eat with my sister and brother. We bought Colton a helium balloon at the restaurant. Well, after the restaurant and a brief stop at a store, as we were getting back into the car, Colton's balloon flew out of his hand and up into the sky. Of course, he cried, so we told him that his balloon went up to Heaven. (After Colton's daddy died, Colton had been told that his daddy lived in Heaven.)

A few days later Colton spent the night with us. He woke up in the morning and the first thing he said was, "I saw daddy last night!"

My other son and I were quite intrigued, so I asked, "What was he doing?"

"Oh, he had a Christmas tree and presents!" (This was in March.)

"Did he have anything to say?"

"Yeah, he said he has my balloon." Then after a very short pause Colton said, "And I want it back!"

There is no doubt in mind that Colton was talking to his daddy and that his daddy took this opportunity to let us know that he was with us at the time that Colton's balloon flew up to Heaven.

—*Patti Hopp*

The Christmas Eve Visit

It was Christmas Eve, and my four-year-old cousin Ethan was at my house, looking at the pictures in my living room. This was the first time he had been over since my husband Kenny had passed away seven months earlier. We felt that Ethan was too young to comprehend that Kenny had died, so we hadn't discussed it with him.

After a while, Ethan pointed to my late husband Kenny's picture. Ethan's mother Nicole told him that it was Uncle Kenny's picture. (Ethan always called my husband Uncle Kenny.) Then a little while later, Ethan was sitting with his mother, Nicole, in the living room on the love seat that faces my dining room. Ethan suddenly pointed upward toward the right corner of the dining room and exclaimed, "Uncle Kenny!"

Nicole corrected him and told him that he was looking at Elmer, Kenny's stepfather, who was sitting about ten feet to the left of where Ethan was pointing.

But Ethan insisted and said, "No, Uncle Kenny!" Again, Ethan was pointing upward to the right corner of the dining room. Nicole and Ethan went back and forth a few times about his seeing his Uncle Kenny. Finally Nicole raised her voice to get him to stop saying that over and over because she was concerned that his talk of seeing Uncle Kenny—my husband—would upset me. After that, Ethan stopped arguing with her and just let it go.

I know Ethan saw Kenny that day. I'm sure of it! I truly believe that my husband Kenny was there with us celebrating with the family. Kenny had always so enjoyed Christmas! I felt his presence all day long as I was cooking. I made all his favorite holiday dishes in honor of him, so I know he was there enjoying it with us.

I believe that Kenny showed himself to Ethan because he knew that Ethan was able to see him and would share it with all of us. I thought this was truly amazing, and it was a very comforting experience for me. I feel blessed to have received this Christmas gift.

—*Cynthia Landrum*

Guilty No More

I would like to share some beautiful spiritual experiences my two-year-old daughter Haley had that were very comforting for us.

Our papaw, James Roland, passed the same week that my daughter Jamie Renee was born. We named her after our papaw. Unfortunately, we were not able to go to James's funeral because it was a far distance from our home, and I was nine months pregnant at the time. My husband and I had been feeling guilty for not being able to say our last good-byes, but we believe that Papaw came back to let us know that it was all right. He did this by appearing to our two-year-old daughter Haley twice the same week that he passed over.

The first time Haley saw our papaw, she said he was outside on our back porch smoking a cigar. The second time that week Haley saw him leaning against my car, and she told me that he said he loved us.

We believed her, and these spiritual visits took away our feelings of guilt and comforted us.

—*Teri Powell*

I Was Living in Mu

My son was a very longed for and wanted little being. I had tried for fifteen years to achieve my dream of having a child. The doctors declared me a useless case and said I should just get on with it.

My beautiful grandmother Dorothy passed over in September 1997, and I began to talk to her daily asking her if she could help me achieve my dream. My exact words were, "Please, Nan, send me a baby." Two months later my baby Cody was on his way, much to my absolute shock and joy.

When Cody was three years old, he would start laughing and talking to "Dot Dot." I asked him to tell me about it and this is his story in his words. "Mummy, Dot Dot is the lady that picked me to come to you. I didn't really want to come because I haven't lived in this world for a very long time. She said it was really important for me to come at this time. I was living in a place called Mu. Some other people who travel with me said I should come here because there are important things I will need to do."

After some research, I found that there is a place named Lemuria, which is referred to as Mu.

When Cody was nine years old, he still remembered his conversations with Dot Dot. He is a highly sensitive child who sees auras around people and knows immediately whether a person has a high-energy vibration. He has meditated and prayed from a very early age. Cody speaks with his guides regularly, and angels often come to visit him in the shape of brightly colored lights.

I believe his contact with his great-grandmother has helped him understand why at times he feels a little different from other children who are not experiencing what he does.

—*Sharon Lee Poultney, Australia*

Dadima

In August 2000 my husband went to visit his mother who lived in Pakistan. After he returned home to the United States, just two months later, sadly, she passed away very unexpectedly.

My daughter Fatima was only two years old at the time. She had never met her grandmother, nor did she understand what death was. Two days after her grandmother's passing, Fatima was in her bed and my husband and I were watching TV. All of a sudden I heard Fatima laughing and talking. I went to see what she was doing. Upon entering the room, I noticed she was sitting up in her bed; her eyes were wide open. She did not even acknowledge the fact that I was there.

"Who are you talking to?" I asked.

"Dadima," she said. (*Dadima* is Arabic for Grandma.)

"Where was she?" I asked. Fatima pointed to the corner of the bed. She was laughing and smiling. "What did she look like?"

"Bright light. Pretty light. Pretty dress," she said.

Another time during that same year my husband was outside changing the oil in his car, and he called me outside to hand him a tool he couldn't reach. When we both came back in, our daughter was running around in circles and laughing. I asked, "What are you doing?"

"I am playing with Dadima."

One day about one year later, my phone rang. I answered it, and much to my surprise, there was a lot of static on the phone. Through the static, I was able to determine that someone was talking on the other end, but I could not make out what the person was saying. I hung up the phone because the connection was so poor. Our daughter asked me why I had hung up on Dadima. I was very surprised that she mentioned Dadima. Shortly afterward the phone rang again. I did not want to answer it because I was feeling a little annoyed and frustrated from the previous unintelligible phone call. In spite of my annoyance, I answered the phone anyway, and this time I distinctly heard my mother-in-law on the other end of the line. She was speaking Arabic, but it was not clear.

I just stood there, not scared, but greatly bewildered. I wondered how she was able to do this. She hung up and so did I.

Fatima asked me what Dadima had said. I told her that I could not understand Dadima, and left the subject alone. After that the visitations became less and less. From time to time, my husband asked, "Where is Dadima?" She said, matter-of-factly, "Dadima is traveling around the world. She told me that she never got to see the world, but now she can."

My husband and I never doubted our daughter. And since that night, my daughter saw her grandmother several times in three years until she was about six years old.

My daughter sees other spirits and talks to them. She is a very gifted child. I encourage her gift and try to help her with it.

—*Lynette, Georgia*

Guess How Much I Love You?

My mom Barbara Ann was Mom Mom to all her grandchildren. My older daughter, Peyton, and my mom had a very special and close relationship. Their favorite story to read together was *Guess How Much I Love You?* by Sam McBratney. At the end of the story the older bunny tucks the little bunny into bed and says, "I love you up to the moon and back."

Every time my mother and Peyton would leave each other, Peyton would say, "Mom Mom, guess how much I love you?" and then quickly follow up with, "I love you up to the moon."

My mom would always say, "But, Peyton, I love you up to the moon and back!"

They always said that to each other.

Sadly, my younger daughter Brynn never got to experience that with my mom. Brynn was only five weeks old when my mom passed from ovarian cancer. Before my mom had passed, she came with me for my baby's ultrasound. From the ultrasound my mom saw that I was having a girl, so I asked her to name the baby. She named her Brynn.

After my mom passed, I bought the hardbound copy of the book *Guess How Much I Love You?* for Brynn. I made two attempts to read it to Brynn but couldn't get past the first page. I would just start to cry and a lump would form in my throat. So I placed the book on Brynn's shelf in her bedroom and left it there for another time when I wasn't so emotional. I didn't know if that time would ever come though.

When Brynn was two and a half years old, we were lying on my bed and I was reading her some stories (but not *Guess How Much I Love You?*). At the end of reading the bedtime stories, I looked at Brynn and suddenly found myself saying to her, "Guess how much I love you?" That was the first time I had ever said those words to Brynn, and she had never heard the story from that particular book because I couldn't bear to read it or even say those words before now.

She just looked at me and stared. I then said, "Up to the moon and back."

Brynn shocked me and said, "Mom Mom always says that to me." I couldn't believe what I heard. I said, "What?"

Brynn repeated, "Mom Mom always says that to me."

"When do you see Mom Mom?"

"When I'm in cribby and going to sleep."

"And you *see* Mom Mom?"

"Yes, you know, *your* mom."

"Yeah, my mom."

And Brynn said, "Yeah, she always tells me that she loves me up to the moon and back."

I knew then, without a doubt, that my mom was visiting Brynn and talking to her. It hurts me so much that she is not physically here to be with Brynn, but I know in my heart she is with her in that special way that is only possible for her to be, and that gives me much comfort.

—*Kim Guido, Pennsylvania*
www.fitkids-challenge.com

Robyn Loves You

My beloved husband, Robyn, passed away in December 2005. It has been two and a half years now, and I believe his spirit has been around my family and me ever since to send us his love and comfort.

My great-niece Alanna was only about a year old at the time of Robyn's passing. One day, a few years later, I was in the kitchen making a cup of coffee when Alanna, who was three and a half years old at the time, came up to me and said words that were a healing balm to my aching heart. She said, "Robyn says he misses you."

I looked at her in amazement and said, "What did you say?"

She repeated it again, and said, "Robyn told me to also tell you that he loves you."

I just about fell over when she told me that. I asked her what made her come to me and tell me that. She explained that she had a dream about Robyn in which he told her to tell me that he misses me and loves me. After she told me this, I gave her a big hug and thanked her. I felt so good after she delivered this beautiful message from Robyn.

I understand kids are more likely to feel the presence of spirits around them than adults do because they're more open than we are. I just have to say how comforting it was that she came up to me and said what she did. Her mother told me that she wouldn't have just told me that if it weren't true and if she didn't really feel she needed to deliver this important message. She knows her daughter can feel Robyn around at times as she's mentioned this to her. There is no doubt that I believe her!

—Julie, California

He Played Trucks with Me

The love of my life, my husband, Daniel Sleep, passed away on December 28, 2008, very unexpectedly of a massive heart attack. My life and all our children's and grandchildren's lives have changed so drastically since he passed over. Dan was one of those guys most people wait their whole lives to meet. He had such a tender loving side under his gruff exterior, was a dynamic full of life guy, was the life of every party, and was a magnet to all children, especially our grandchildren.

I hadn't given much thought about death or about what happens to us after we die before he passed, and I hadn't even heard of ADCs or anything of that sort. So needless to say, receiving afterlife contacts has been a very enlightening and learning experience for my family and me. Although we miss him so very much, we're all very aware of his "presence" in our lives. Each of us has heard from Dan in such unique ways. God bless him!

A week after Dan passed, my daughter Lindsey and I sat down to watch the video that was shown at Dan's funeral. The video showed pictures of Dan starting with him as an infant all the way up to just before he passed. As we sat watching the video, pictures of Dan when he was three years old were showing on the screen when our two-year-old grandson, Aikley, walked into the room. He looked at the TV and said, "Mom, that is Papa."

Lindsey said, "Yes, sweetie, that is Papa."

I sat there dumbfounded, thinking about what had just happened. I turned to my daughter and said, "How in the world would he know that childhood photo was of Dan?"

Lindsey got this puzzled look on her face and said, "Wow, how would he know that, Mom?" You see, Lindsey did not take Aikley to Dan's funeral, so he had not seen this particular video before, nor had he seen pictures of Dan when Dan was only three years old.

That was our first incident with Aikley and Papa Dan!

I always knew they had a "special" relationship as my daughter had lived with us when Aikley was born. From the first day Aikley came home, Dan bonded with him. As Aikley grew, they were always together playing or talking, and whenever they parted, Aikley said, "Love you, Papa," as he hugged him.

Of course, Dan replied, "Love you too, buddy!"

The second incident was in February, as my daughter Lindsey was getting ready to go to work at 5:30 in the morning. Lindsey and Aikley were the only two awake in the house. Aikley was sitting on the kitchen carpet trying to get dressed to go to the babysitter's when Lindsey heard him laughing out loud. As she walked into the room, Aikley was still laughing, and he said, "Papa is getting my socks, Mom."

With a confused look, Lindsey asked, "You mean Papa Jeff?"

Aikley replied, "No, Papa Dan, see him, Mom? He is right there by the light."

Aikley was pointing to the light by the sink. Lindsey was somewhat afraid to turn and look at where he was pointing, but at the same time, she almost expected to see Dan standing there. When she did finally look, she didn't see anyone.

As they went out to the car and were getting ready to leave, Aikley asked his mom, "Where is Papa? Isn't he coming?"

Lindsey turned and looked at him and said, "Sweetie, Papa Dan is in Heaven. He is far, far away."

Aikley adamantly said, "No, Mom, he is in the kitchen, he is *not* far, far away. He is by the light!" Lindsey was so overwhelmed that she cried.

The third incident was on Aikley's third birthday on March 10, 2009. He said, "Papa came and played with me, Granny."

"Oh, honey, that is so wonderful. Did he wish you a happy birthday?"

"No, he told me he loved me." Then Aikley raised his little arm, making a fist with his small hand, and said, "He's gonna punch me in the kisser!"

I was so elated with this reply, for I had watched them play so many times and make this special "gesture" to each other. Aikley would teasingly do it to Dan, and, of course, Dan would make a fist and say those very words back to Aikley as they both laughed out loud.

As Aikley sat on my lap telling me about his "talk" with Papa, Aikley asked, "Where is Heaven?"

"Heaven is above us."

"Heaven is *not* far, far away, Granny!"

Of course, I did not argue, for I tend to believe he knows much more than I do about Heaven now.

The fourth incident happened in April 2009. My nineteen-year-old daughter, Holly, had just gotten engaged and was crying as she commented on how she so wished Dan could be at her wedding. I told her without a blink of an eye that he wouldn't miss it; he will be there! The very next morning, I got a call at work from Holly. She was sobbing as she said, "Mom, Dan just visited me in my dream and it was so real!"

This got my undivided attention!

She said she walked into the living room and Dan was sitting in his rocking chair with Aikley on one knee and our nine-year-old-son, Cody, on the other knee. She asked Dan what he was doing here, and he replied, "Well, Aikley and I just got done playing trucks outside." He continued to tell Holly that he was very proud of her, that her engagement ring was so beautiful, and that she didn't need to worry about him not being at the wedding, because he wouldn't miss it for the world! (Dan had no way of knowing about the wedding or the ring, for she got engaged after he passed.)

Holly started crying in the dream and said, "I miss you so much and I am worried about you!"

"Don't worry about me, I am in a good place!" At that instance, Holly woke up.

Now I was so amazed at Holly's dream and thought about it most of the day. So that evening, when I saw Aikley, I asked him, without mentioning any specifics, "Aikley, did Papa Dan come see you yesterday?"

He smiled a great big smile and said, "Yep, he played trucks with me outside!"

Now, I am not a genius, but I can tell you without a shadow of a doubt that Aikley's answer was absolute "proof" that Papa Dan is here among us, watching, listening, and still playing with the children! Oh, how happy that makes me!

—*Sonia Smith, Iowa*
danielsleep.virtual-memorials.com

Look, Can You See My Daddy?

My granddaughter Amanda was only two and a half years old when her daddy (my son) passed away on January 14, 2005. We have noticed that there are times when she still seems to see and talk to him.

Amanda started day care when she was around two years old because both parents worked. Mark would stop by the day care center just to look through the window and see her. The teachers would tell Amanda's mother that Mark was the only father who did that. He was able to do that because he was an A/C Tech and was always in the area of the center.

A year after her daddy passed, she was playing outside at her day care and the teacher aide noticed Amanda was walking off toward some trees. She was concerned that Amanda was walking away, so she quickly went over to Amanda to bring her back to the rest of the children. When the teacher aide reached my little granddaughter, Amanda said to her, "Look, can you see my daddy?" The aide looked toward the trees but couldn't see anything. The aide hadn't known that Amanda's daddy had passed away, so she naturally thought that perhaps he'd come by to look in on her and then left. The aide continued to talk with Amanda who didn't want to leave the tree area. After a while, she finally convinced Amanda to join the other children.

When Claudia, Amanda's mother, arrived to pick up Amanda, the teacher told her about what had happened. Claudia informed the teacher that Amanda's daddy had passed away. The teacher was stunned and a little shaken upon hearing that news. Later when Claudia was alone with Amanda, she asked if she had seen Daddy on the playground. Without hesitation, Amanda said, "Yes mommy, I saw Daddy over by the trees, and he kept waving at me."

My son's name was Mark Anthony and we miss him so much. It didn't surprise me that my son dropped in on his little daughter from the afterlife as this was something he often did in life.

Hearing that he visits his daughter has brought us a tremendous amount of peace in our lives. God bless.

—*Maureen Leon, Florida*

Amy's Guardian Angel

Amy Cameron Wiard was born October 20, 1989. She came into the world in a hurry with a short labor and a "ha!" This seemed like a laugh, a celebration of birth and life. She continued with this celebration of life and a loving heart for all who she came in contact with and left her contagious radiating heart beating within their own hearts.

In February of 1991 Amy's mom, Leslie Wiard, became sick and was quickly admitted to the hospital. More and more Amy found herself sleeping over at her grandparents' homes. Within a week, Amy was baptized and her parents talked to both Amy and her older sister, Keri (age three at the time) to let them know their mother was sick with cancer. She had sarcomatoid renal cell carcinoma. At this time no one had lived with this form of cancer for longer than seven weeks and the person was usually over the age of seventy, yet Amy's mom was only 28 years old. Soon Amy found her mom in the hospital for surgeries, chemotherapy, and other treatments for her cancer. Amy's mom seemed gone more than at home, and when she was home, quite often she was very sick. Still her mom always found time to show her love and allow Amy to feel special.

One day in March 1991, as her dad was putting her to bed, she asked him if he saw the man in the corner of the room. Her dad became nervous as this seemed like a pretty serious mental issue. Could this be the stress of her mom's illness or her mom being away quite often for treatments? Was Dad being a bad dad? Had his daughter been molested or something? He did not know, but he was concerned.

He sat down beside his little girl and, without wanting to squelch his daughter's vision, started asking some questions. What does this "man" look like? Where is he? Does he scare you? The answers were straightforward.

Amy giggled at her father and stated, "Dad, can't you see him? He is an Indian chief, with big feathers for a headdress, a soft face with a reverent look of piercing eyes, large nose, and pierced, yet loving, lips."

Amy was not old enough, being just over two years, to use such mature words; it was clear this Indian chief was giving Amy the words to say to me. This chief gave her safety and security in a time when all of that was being eroded with each medical test.

Her dad, who was a schoolteacher at the time, went to school the next day and told Amy's preschool teacher, Michelle, about the vision Amy had. Michelle was a tall Jamaican woman with a strong and silent presence. Michelle could see the worry in the face of Amy's dad and took him aside. She told him of her belief that children come into this world without the "adult filters" that stop them from seeing spirits and with the ability to communicate or share with the other side of the veil. For some reason this made sense to her dad as Amy did not seem afraid and actually seemed to feel safe having this chief in her bedroom. Her small family home was built on a mesa that was filled with pottery shards, arrowheads, and other evidence of past communities that had once lived on the same mesa. Somehow, it all made sense and put Amy's dad at ease.

Gently and quietly Amy's chief continued to stay with her every night for the next two years just sitting in the corner, allowing Amy to feel safe, grounded, and held by something bigger than her parents and her grandparents—and something so much larger than anyone could ever know. Amy was held within the security of the other side for two years. When her dad checked in, Amy would just seem so amazed that her silly dad couldn't see him, trust him, and feel the safety that radiated out into the room. It was like Amy's cocoon in the midst of a very sad story happening right outside her bedroom door.

On February 8, 1993, Amy's mother died after a heroic and amazing dance with her cancer. As her mother stated, each family member was being reborn in this death/birth process and that was what was now happening.

Soon after her mom had died and the funeral and ceremonies

were over, the home became healthy once again but with a large void of a missing mom. One evening there was a ceremony in which the house was "smudged" using sage and juniper (as well as prayers). The entire house was "cleansed" of sickness, cancer, and exhaustion. During the ceremony right at sunset with the front door open, an enormous gust of wind came flying through the house blowing open the backdoor, making all the blinds shutter radically as well as the pictures swing and the tennis rackets fall off the racket stringer. The front door slammed shut and then all was quiet. What a freaky moment!

That night Amy seemed tearful and tired as her dad sat down at the side of her bed; Amy looked over at him and said, "Daddy, he's gone. My chief is gone." Amy was never to see her spirit guide again. Possibly the ceremony, or the death of her mom, or her age was the reason why the veil had closed, and Amy no longer saw the other side except through her long evening talks to her mother as she looked up to her "Mommy Star" that was the morning star.

Both Amy and her sister Keri continued to grow with their dad, learning to live a life as a family of three. Yet for Amy, it was as if her mom had taken the chief's place. Even though Amy could not see her mom, she knew she was held and loved at all times by her mom. Somehow her dad missed the chief as he had been her "blanky" and now he was gone, just like Mom. Amy seemed secure even if Dad did not.

Time moved forward, and before long it was the summer of 1996. Amy and Keri had gone to visit their aunt in Denver. After their trip, they spent the night at their maternal grandparents' home as their father was in Albuquerque, New Mexico, coaching his tennis team. The next day while their grandmother was driving them back to their home to meet up with the babysitter, she went through an intersection and was sideswiped by a trash truck with Amy and her grandmother dying instantly and Keri living for a day. All of a sudden her father found himself alone, stripped and jealous of the chief who now held Amy and was with her as well as her sister and mother.

As time went by, Amy's father tried to rebuild his life and to the best of his ability heal from his losses. One of the vehicles used for healing was ceremonies, especially Native American ceremonies such as sweat lodges, prayer ties, and guided journeys in which the mind is allowed to wander into the subconscious and enter into the realm of the unknown. What happened during these ceremonies, as well as guided imagery, hypnotherapy, and good old dreaming, is the chief reappeared to her father, and now in most ceremonies of any type, the chief is there coaching him, letting him know there is a bigger picture and allowing him to go on with his life knowing he is being held by the spiritual universe.

Thanks, Amy, for sharing your guide with your dad, and in that, the world at large.

—Rev. Ted Wiard, New Mexico
www.goldenwillowretreat.org

Grandma's Talking! Grandma's Talking!

My mom died in August of 2008. She was only fifty-eight years old. My youngest child had just turned two years old a month before that. When my mom died, I explained it to my older kids that their grandma had died, but didn't really say very much to my two-year-old daughter because I didn't think she would understand what it meant to die. In my grief and sorrow, I still tried to be as normal as I could around her so that she wouldn't think anything was wrong.

Well, in the days that followed my mom's death, my two-year-old wasn't sleeping very well. She would wake up and cry more often than usual. After a few days of this, I was so weary that I gave up and brought her downstairs to sleep with me in my bed, since my husband was not home. I was very tired, but my daughter was wide awake talking and babbling on and on. I tried ignoring her.

"Grandma's talking," she said.

I continued to try to go back to sleep.

"Mommy! Mommy! Do you hear that? Grandma's talking!" she said more urgently.

I then asked her what Grandma was saying, but she didn't answer me. Then she smiled and looked toward the corner of the room like she saw something there. She changed the subject and started talking about babies and bears and all the normal things that she usually talks about.

For months after that, every time we went to Grandma's house, she would ask where Grandma was because she didn't understand that she'd died and still expected to see her there. It wasn't until perhaps six months later that she began to understand that Grandma was not here any longer, but was in Heaven with Jesus. That night it was both weird and remarkable that my daughter heard someone talking in my room when nobody else was in the house but the two of us. I believe my daughter was genuinely talking to my mother.

—*Michelle*

Friend or Foe?

It was September 1985. We were living in Holland, Pennsylvania, right behind St. Bede's Roman Catholic Church. My daughter Blaire was two years old at the time, and my son was eight months old. The first sign of a spiritual presence was when we noticed that everyone in the house had items missing: Blaire's little pink socks, my son's favorite toy, my husband's important work papers, my house keys, and a special head of Christ medal from Italy. I felt there was a spirit in the house, as all these articles could not just have disappeared on their own.

There would be knocks on our front door during the most inopportune times, and when we answered the door, no one would be there. Another strange sign of a spirit's presence would be someone knocking at our front door using our door knocker, yet our screen door was always locked. Somehow the spirit was able to bypass our screen door. Items would be moved in the house from one room to the next and our coffee pot would just turn on by itself right before I was about to make a pot of coffee. Our house was always cold even with the heat turned up, and there always seemed to be a scent of oregano throughout the house.

I called a friend who was a priest living at St. Charles Borromeo Seminary, and I explained the situation to him. Trust me, this is the honest to God's truth. While talking to him on the phone, our phone connection was all jumbled and not clear. There was so much static and interference on the phone line that we could barely hear one another. It was as if some unseen force were blocking our trying to communicate with each other. The only thing I was able to hear him say was that, yes, it seems as if there's a spirit in the house, he's a prankster, he won't hurt you, and he'd be up to bless the house soon. So be it. We waited and hoped his visit would be soon.

Strangely enough, my priest friend at the seminary became very ill after our initial phone call and was sick in bed for three months. After his recuperation, he and his friend made plans to drive to our house to say some special prayers. Oddly enough, on their way to the house they got lost, which was very peculiar because they'd visited us several times. They had to resort to knocking on doors on our street just to find us. When they finally arrived, they were both disoriented and didn't even recognize us at first. Strange, isn't it? Once there they proceeded to bless the house and to pray for an hour in Blaire's bedroom.

The night following the initial phone conversation with my priest friend, we put Blaire to bed at her usual time. For some reason she woke up crying hysterically and was pointing to the corner of her bedroom, saying that John was here. We didn't know a John, so I immediately became concerned. After we calmed her down a bit, we brought her downstairs and let her play for a while. The whole time she was playing, she was talking to John saying things like, "Mom, please tell John to stop pulling my hair," and carrying on a full conversation with this person she called John. Blaire's conversations with John continued from September to November.

One time we were at the mall shopping, and she pointed to a young man and said, "There's John." The young man she was pointing to had long hair and was wearing a T-shirt and jeans. Later on, I, too, was awakened during the night to find the same type of young man standing at the foot of my bed.

I was getting very uncomfortable with all of this. It just so happened that it was around Halloween, and there was an article in our local newspaper about the University of Pennsylvania's parapsychology department. So I called the department and asked for advice. The people I spoke to said that obviously this spirit had connected with Blaire for some reason. Their suggestion was to burn sage in Blaire's bedroom and to crack the window a little so that when the spirit departed, the glass in the window wouldn't crack. I followed their advice.

The day I tried this was warm with no breeze. As the sage was burning, much to my surprise, a wind blew in through the screen causing the meshing to buckle in toward the room, but as I said, it wasn't a windy or breezy day. I took it as a sign that this spirit wasn't going anywhere.

I called the parapsychology department again and explained what happened. They said to try one more thing, and if that didn't work, they would come to the house. They said to get sea salt and sprinkle it all around the perimeter of the rooms in the house saying the "Our Father" prayer. The night I went out to purchase the sea salt, it was pouring rain, roads were flooded, and the health food store was closed when I got there.

I was able to purchase the salt the following day. I did as I was told, sprinkling the salt in all corners of all the rooms saying the "Our Father" prayer. Immediately afterward, the house warmed up and the thermostat read eighty degrees. I found some of the missing articles on the steps: the pink socks, toy, and keys. Then, to my utter amazement, the unplugged light in my foyer went on! I felt that this spirit called John came down the steps and left through the front door.

We wound up moving to Bensalem, Pennsylvania, the following year, and I just happened to run into someone who lived in Holland and said he was very friendly with many people who lived there. I told him where I had lived and the house address. He said he was best friends with the person who used to live in our house—a person by the name of "Jack" (which is a nickname for John) who had a two-year-old daughter, and, unfortunately, Jack was killed in an accident in Philadelphia a few years back. I said, "I never knew Jack, but the spirit had long hair, wore jeans and a T-shirt."

"That's Jack. Always in his jeans and a T-shirt, needing a haircut," he said.

Now that blew my mind! Now everything made sense. I believe that Jack or John, as Blaire called him, was coming back to his house to visit his daughter who was the same age as my daughter.

For the next two years, Blaire at ages three and four would ask to go back to the house and play with the man named John, but she would only ask during the months of September and October. Her behavior in school would become erratic during those months as well, and I would tell her teacher that she will calm down come November—and she did every time.

My daughter is now an adult and does not remember any of this. But I will never forget it.

—*Maryanne, Pennsylvania*

Christmas Day

My father, Don Brady, was close to my three-year-old niece, Brenna, and would always read books to her and spend a lot of time talking with her whenever she came over to visit him. She was very special to him. It was clear that she loved being around him too! After my father passed away, Brenna missed his presence, but did not understand that he had passed. She would only talk about him occasionally, and when asked about him, she would say that Grandpa was sick and at the hospital. This is what we had told her to help her understand why he was not around.

Every Christmas, my brothers and I would bring our families to our parents' house to exchange presents and to have dinner together. The first Christmas following my father's death was especially hard for all of us. We missed him so. However, something strange but wondrous happened. Brenna looked out the living room window and spontaneously exclaimed so excitedly and joyfully, "Grandpa's here!" We looked, but we adults did not have the ability to see through the veil the way Brenna did. My dad was very much alive to Brenna because he appeared to her.

Later that same day, while handing out presents, I handed one to Brenna. As she took it from me, she asked, "Is it from Grandpa?" She said this even though no one had been talking about him. I believe there was a reason why she thought the present was from him. I couldn't help but wonder if she had seen my father in the room just then too. Perhaps he showed himself to her again, just like earlier in the day when he appeared to her outside of the living room window.

Brenna brought great relief to me that day, since it was my first Christmas without my dad. Brenna's spiritual sighting gave me hope that Dad was spending Christmas Day with us again.

—*Crissy Brady, Wisconsin*

Daddy's House in Heaven

My twenty-year-old son, Justin, was tragically and unexpectedly killed in an automobile accident in December 2004. My son left us a beautiful grandson named Colton. Colton has spoken of seeing his daddy a number of times, starting when he was two years old.

On one occasion when Colton was four years old, he was riding in the backseat of our car. My sister and I were in the front talking to each other. Out of nowhere Colton blurted out, "I saw my daddy's house."

I asked, "You mean *my* house?"

"No! His house is in heaven! There was a *huge* slide, a pool, a ping-pong table, and a baseball field!"

My son Justin and my nephew Tony, who died in the same accident, both loved playing ping-pong.

I said, "Wow, that was a nice dream you had."

Colton, almost offended by my comment about it being a dream, corrected me and said, "It *wasn't* a dream, Grandma. He showed me for real!"

Justin loved all those activities. I honestly believe that Justin showed Colton where he lived in Heaven. Since it was not a dream, I believe it was a heavenly vision that was given to little Colton. Innocent children have the ability to see heaven, perhaps because they have recently traveled from there and God has allowed them to keep that ability for a while. I believe their openness and purity is the key.

—*Patti Hopp*

The Ball Goes Right Through Buddy

When Josh was born in April 1990, he had medical problems and sadly died at the age of four years old in June 1994.

His cousin Jayden, my grandson, was born on June 9, 2005, and began playing with Josh on June 30, 2007, at the age of two.

The Josh/Buddy Encounters

When Jayden first saw "Buddy," he was at Myrtle Beach, South Carolina. He would play with him, and he would even force people to move if they started to sit where Buddy was sitting. He told his mom-mom that Buddy's dead; he lives up there and pointed to the sky. When finally asked if Buddy had a name, he said, "Josh." Everyone was stunned, because Jayden was born eleven years after Josh had died!

Upon returning home from Myrtle Beach, Jayden's mother Ashley rummaged around and found two pictures she had of Josh. They were in black and white. She showed them to Jayden to see what her little two-year-old would say. Jayden said that the boy in one of the pictures was Josh. The other picture of Josh was on his memorial card. When Jayden saw it, he said, "That's Buddy. He's dead. Lives up there."

And Jayden pointed upward. Yet no one had told Jayden about Josh or even talked about death in front of him. Buddy and Josh were obviously one and the same spirit.

Jayden knew other facts about Josh/Buddy. For instance, once when Jayden was chewing, he was asked what was in his mouth. He answered, "Bananas. Buddy loves bananas." He was right. That was Josh's favorite food.

Jayden told us that Buddy loved fireworks—-and he did. He told us that Buddy had curly yellow hair. Which was also true. However, the pictures of Josh that were shown to Jayden were only in black and white. So there was no way Jayden would have known that his hair was blond without actually having personally seen him.

A friend of the family owns a motorcycle, and one day he rode over on his bike to visit. While he was there, Jayden looked up and said that Buddy was here. He then added, "That's Buddy's daddy's old bike." Amazingly, he was right again! When Josh was alive, Josh's father owned that same bike, but at that time it had been a different color with different markings. Josh's father has not been part of the family for a long time, so Jayden would not have known about the bike ownership connection either.

One day when the kids were outside playing, a swing was moving all by itself, and Jayden told everyone that Buddy was there.

Another time, at a high school football game with his mother, his grandmother, Josh's mother Brenda, and the half sister of Josh, Jayden suddenly got excited and said, "Buddy's here!" He said he was standing behind Brenda.

For a while, Buddy was bringing two friends that we never were able to identify, but they all played together. Once when the three spirits and Jayden were playing in Jayden's room, Jayden told Buddy that the Xbox was in the other room. Then he asked his mom for three more controllers so that they could all play!

In April 2009, when Jayden was four years old, he told us that it was Buddy's birthday, and we had to get him a birthday cake. Jayden was right. Josh/Buddy had been born in the month of April in 1990.

Jayden and his mother attended a wedding several months ago, and Jayden said, "Buddy's daddy's here." He was right. Josh's dad was there. This was a rare occurrence for his dad to be around. And Jayden had never met him.

Jayden now has a little brother Kade. Once when Kade was laughing, Jayden told his mother that Buddy was making him laugh.

One time down at Myrtle Beach, Jayden, who was four years old at the time, and his mother were throwing a football around. Ashley was getting tired, so she said why don't you play with Buddy? Jayden said he already tried to, but that the ball went right through him!

If you ask Jayden where Buddy is, he will tell you, "In the clouds."

The Fellow Encounters

Recently, Jayden and his family moved to a house that is connected to a restaurant/pub owned by his soon-to-be stepfather Shane. One day while Jayden was driving in the car, he started singing, "There's a ghost in the pub house." Jayden now talks to "Fellow." It turns out that a man named John used to live in the house and died there in July 2007. When they showed Jayden a picture of John, he said it was Fellow. He said he sees Fellow standing at the end of the bar. Apparently, that is where John always stood. Jayden told Shane that Fellow was very close to him, which he was.

Jayden's encounters with these loving spirits have been validated by the information the spirits have been giving Jayden to relay to us. I believe they do this so that we will believe him. They have been a tremendous source of comfort for the family and we hope that Jayden will have the ability to continue seeing and hearing spirits for the rest of his life.

—*Marianne Kohn, Pennsylvania*

Guardie

Rob was a close family friend since my brother and I were in high school. A tall strapping lad, with a great sense of humor, he loved children and animals. Every year he and my brother would ride their bikes up to Laconia, New Hampshire, for a motorcycle weekend. We shared many summer days at the beach and winter nights drinking eggnog and skating on thin ice.

In the early 1990s, Rob was diagnosed with a brain tumor. After several surgeries and chemotherapy, the cancer went into remission. Shortly thereafter Rob and Tara married. My brother John was the best man at their wedding, and Rob returned the favor the following year when John married his fiancée Donna.

One weekend in early 1994, while Rob and Tara were in Maine, Rob suffered a seizure. Testing revealed that his cancer had returned. During the months that followed, he was constantly in and out of the hospital. I visited as often as I could. Sometimes on the nights before I planned on visiting, I'd cook up a batch of his favorite pasta with white clam sauce so he wouldn't have to exist solely on hospital food. The nurses on his floor always knew when I'd arrived by the pungent smell of garlic wafting through the halls.

My sister-in-law Donna was pregnant with my niece, Jonna, in November 1994. We visited Rob in the hospital on Thanksgiving Day that year, and I'll never forget how his face brightened with joy when John and Donna told him the news about the new baby.

The following January, after a long, brave battle, Rob died. And six months later on July 23 (what would have been Rob's twenty-eighth birthday), my niece Jonna was born.

At first none of us paid too much mind to Jonna's imaginary friend, Guardie. After all, plenty of kids have imaginary friends. But one night when her nana was babysitting and her parents headed off for a ride on the motorcycle, she piqued Nana's interest.

"Nana! Guardie is leaving on the motorcycle with Mommy and Daddy. He never does that. He always stays here to take care of me and Mikey!"

"What does Guardie look like?" Nana asked.

"He's a skeleton, a man skeleton, and he's tall, taller than Daddy," she replied.

Later that evening when John and Donna returned home and Nana told them what Jonna said, they began to have their suspicions about Guardie.

Rob's wife Tara and I have remained close through the years, and she'd often join me for a workout in my downstairs gym. One Tuesday evening she stayed for dinner after our workout. When I complimented her on the shirt she was wearing, she told me that it was Rob's, and we both paused for a moment in melancholy reflection. Later while we were having dinner, my dining room light dimmed by itself. No big deal. I went to turn it back up and my hand was still at least a foot away from the switch when the light suddenly brightened. That was when we panicked.

"Christine, you didn't even touch it," Tara whispered.

"I know," I said, grabbing for my white sage and frantically lighting it while commanding the dark entity to be gone. I abruptly stopped when I realized that it was probably Rob popping in for a whiff of my famous guacamole. "Never mind, come back," I cried. But he already had his fun.

The following Saturday night, I went to my brother's house for fondue dinner. John was upstairs playing with Jonna and Mikey, and I was in the kitchen with Donna and her sister Katie telling them about the light dimming and brightening on its own when Tara was over on Tuesday. I had already finished the story when four-year-old Jonna walked in. She looked at me and her jaw dropped.

"Auntie! Guardie is sitting right on top of your head!" she cried excitedly. So I picked her up, snuggled her, and sat her on the kitchen counter.

"Would you ask him if he came to visit Auntie at her house one night this week?"

She sat on the counter swinging her little legs and looking at the space above my head. "Guardie, did you visit Auntie at her house this week?" After a short pause she told me that Guardie said yes, he did visit me.

"Could you ask him if he remembers what night it was that he came over?" I pressed. She repeated my question, and after another short pause, told me that Guardie said he visited me on Tuesday. My heart pounded with joy. Even though this was the validating answer that I was hoping for, a shiver ran down my spine and my eyes welled up with tears of happiness and gratitude. That experience was a priceless gift that forever cleared any doubt from my mind about whether physical death is really the end.

—*Christine Casoli, Massachusetts*

Elmer

My granddaughter Leah began communications with "Elmer" when she was about three and a half years old. It was right after her mother, my daughter, moved out and left Leah and her sister with their father. She moved out without telling them that she was leaving.

Two years ago I stayed overnight with the girls at their home. We had a girls' night. Leah said, "Grandma, if you wake up and see an old man in the corner, it's just Elmer. He's here to watch over us and not let anything happen to us. So don't be scared, okay?"

We never could connect Elmer with anyone in our family, so we thought that perhaps Elmer was the name of Leah's guardian angel.

My oldest daughter Julie (Leah's aunt) passed away from cancer two years ago. Leah and her sister came to visit me about three weeks after her death. We were talking one night, and she came up to me and put her arms around me and said, "I know you feel so bad that Julie died, but I want you to know she is okay and will always be here with you." She was seven years old at the time.

To me, Leah is like a seventy-year-old lady in a little girl's body. She is so matter of fact and very outspoken. Leah's dad encourages her gift. I am so happy that he does. Leah's great-grandmother had the same gift.

—*Denise Forry, Minnesota*

Their Special Circles

They met when she was literally a babe in her mother's arms. She was less than two months old; he was nineteen. She was the light and love of his life. In their two years together, they shared love, laughter, and blue eyes.

When my niece Marie was a small child and cried out to be held, her uncle Matt, my brother, was the one who brought her peace and comfort. He was able to soothe her when no one else could. It was the gift he shared with her. Together the world fell away and nothing and no one else existed.

Matt went away to college to complete his education. He died that fall right after her second birthday. He was twenty-one; she was two years and twenty-one days old. The entire family was devastated by the loss, except for the young child. She knew something was wrong, someone was missing, but couldn't express it.

No matter where she went, ever present were swirls of circles. They appeared everywhere, in the fallen leaves, in her sandbox, and in the toys in her playroom. They all formed into circles. The circles followed her childhood. If she had a sad time or moment, she would find something in the shape of a circle and go to the middle of it.

At one point, I visited my niece when she was four; she was babbling amidst a circle of blocks.

"Marie, who are you talking to?" I asked as I seated myself outside of the circle.

"It's Matt. He plays with me when I'm sad," she said. "Sometimes I play with him when he's sad."

"Are you sad today, sweetie?"

"No, but he is."

"Can you see him?"

She smiled. "You're silly. Of course I can see him."

"Okay. Tell me what he looks like."

She described my brother Matt just as he'd looked the last time my brother and I had been together. From the color of his hair to his glasses, even the fact that he always wore jewel-toned plaid shirts. She described him as though she'd seen him in a picture. I had taken that picture. It lived in my scrapbook that I never shared with anyone.

"Is he sad very much?" I asked.

"No," she replied.

"But you said he comes when you are sad or he is," I said.

Marie explained further, "Well, he also comes when I ask him to come. He plays games with me."

Matt did have infinite patience with small children and games and their lack of rules.

As she aged, my sister told me that Matt came by less and less but that Marie still talked about him. He was more real to her than her stepbrother and stepsister. He was a constant friend. He was her confidant in all things.

When she was twelve, she wanted to learn to dance. She chose ballet, of course, because so many of the foot patterns made circles. The fact that the tutus were a big attraction meant nothing, it was all about the feet and turning in a circle whenever possible. After her one and only recital, I asked "Was it a good evening?"

"It was perfect." She gushed about the entire experience and the amount of work it had been. It seemed that the work involved was enough to make her decide to give up a dream of dance long term. "Do you know what made it amazing?" she asked.

"No, what made it amazing?"

"Matt was in the front row. I could see his smile from the stage."

She then adjusted her body so she was arranged just the way he used to sit. Her smile even looked like his; it haunted me for days. I was thrilled to see the smile again; I'd forgotten just how much I'd missed it.

"Do you still talk to him?" I asked. I hoped she did and that he wasn't just an imaginary friend when she was so very, very young.

"Sure," she said.

It seemed that they talked about everything: school, boys, and horses. Also, the place she wanted to go to learn to ride horses trained in a riding ring, again with the circle.

When she turned sixteen, I asked her what she wanted for a sweet sixteen gift. She wanted a pendant that had a circle on it; they were just coming into fashion.

"Marie, what is the significance of the circle?" I asked. I'd wanted to ask for years, but I didn't want to hear that it was a coincidence.

"Aunt Lisa," she said looking at me like I was a bit of a dim bulb, "all of life is a circle. We are born, we live, we die, we see our loved ones again. Everyone is part of the circle, just because we don't see them doesn't mean they aren't there."

About the time of this "great revelation" as I thought of it, my other sister had twins, Anne and Steven. As infants, they had amazing personalities, always laughing and smiling. I wonder just how often my brother stopped by to play with them because they have also been drawn to circles.

—*Lisa Fisk, Arizona*

The Angel Kids

When my daughter Peyton was two and a half years old, I took my grandmother and her for a visit to Resurrection Cemetery. My grandmother wanted to visit the grave of her great-grandchild. He was a stillborn baby. His name was Angel. Once we arrived at the site, I removed Peyton from her car seat and let her stand outside the car. In the process of assisting my elderly grandmother out of the car, Peyton took off running and yelling loudly, "Mom, I'm going to play with all of the little angels."

She was so excited and happy. Picture this, I'm assisting my elderly grandmother and trying not to take my eyes off of my grandmother because she was a little unstable. I looked up to see where Peyton ran to and saw her dancing around a nearby tree as if playing the musical game ring-around-the-rosy. My grandmother asked where did she go. I repeated what she said to me about going to play with all the little angels. My grandmother said, "Oh she must mean Angel."

My grandmother and I slowly walked to the place where Peyton was playing, and Peyton looked up at us, then looked back at the tree and said, "Where did all of the angels go?"

I asked, "Did you mean Angel?"

"No Mommy, all of the angel kids. They were playing with me. They were my friends."

At the time, we happened to be in the section of Resurrection Cemetery where all the kids were buried.

—*Kim Guido, Pennsylvania*

Irish Catholic

After the tragic death of our twenty-five-year-old son, Eric, my husband Fred, our other son Scott, and I had three separate visits to see a psychic medium or seer, which we found to be very helpful in our healing process.

Three years after Eric's untimely death, my husband and I met a woman who was a newspaper reporter for the *Avon Lake Press* in Avon Lake, Ohio. My husband had read that she was going to be doing a series of articles about mediums to get the "truth" about them. So Fred called her to tell her about our experiences.

The reporter was interested in our story and came to interview us. We could tell she didn't believe in mediums or "any of that kind of stuff." She was Irish Catholic and she asked tough questions. We finally convinced her to go to a woman named Eleanor for a reading. She agreed and phoned Eleanor to set up a meeting. When the reporter requested a reading, she only gave her first name. She received an appointment about two weeks later. We knew this would be an interesting event because of the reporter's background and her belief system. The fact that Eleanor was also Catholic made it even more interesting. Two opposing beliefs but the same religion!

After the reading, the reporter came to see us again, this time full of amazement. She was smiling. Gone was that tough reporter exterior she had when we first met. She said she now was a believer because a couple of days after she had called for the appointment and before she even went for the reading, her three-year-old daughter did something that truly amazed her. From out of the blue, her daughter walked into the kitchen and started calling her Woman. "Woman, get me my breakfast!" "Woman, where are my shoes?"

The reporter was astonished at this particular name because her grandmother, who had been dead over ten years and had never met her daughter or even her husband, was the only person who used that name Woman when referring to her. Curious, the reporter questioned her little daughter and asked, "Why are you calling me Woman instead of Mommy or Mom?"

Her little daughter replied, "It's because that lady who comes into my bedroom at night and talks to me calls you that all the time."

Then the reporter told them that when she went for her reading about a week later, her grandmother came through, and Eleanor, the medium, told her all kinds of things about her and her family. She said the grandmother had been visiting her little daughter to get her ready for this moment in her life.

Well, my husband Fred and I both smiled and said, "You see, there are things in this world that you can't explain and yet you believe because it has happened to you."

We had a great talk, and she told us how this had changed her life immensely. She thanked us for showing her this part of life. She felt comforted and was happier than she had ever been in her life.

Eleanor, who prefers to be called a seer and not a medium, lives in Avon Lake, Ohio. She has literally helped thousands of people over the years coping with the loss of a loved one via her mediumship abilities and concern and love for mankind.

—*Marilyn and Fred Zimmerman, North Carolina*

CHAPTER 3

Afterlife Encounters
Children Five to Nine Years Old

This chapter contains thirty-three delightful stories of children ages five to nine years old who reported seeing and talking to spirits of loved ones, pets, angels, and Jesus. The children understood the meaning of death and, in many cases, were aware that the person who visited them had died. They and their families derived a great deal of comfort and peace from their experiences.

The Halo

In August 2005, my only brother Patrick was killed in a still unsolved, but suspected, homicide. At the time of his death, my three sons were seven years, three years, and four weeks old. Before going to bed each night, my sons and I pray together, always simple children's prayers, giving thanks for the blessings of the day and praying to God to keep our loved ones safe and happy. The final thing we pray for is that the police will be brave, safe, and able to gain the knowledge to figure out what happened to their Uncle Pat. My children do not know that he was murdered; they only know that he was involved in an accident that most likely involved some bad guys.

My two oldest sons both have had experiences with my brother

Pat since he died, as have I. About two months after my brother died, my oldest son, Brett, who had just turned eight years old, was in his bed, and I leaned over to give him a hug and a kiss goodnight. The room was dark. As I stood up to leave the room he said, "Mom, I wonder how Uncle Pat feels about that thing around his head."

I asked, "What do you mean?"

He said, "You know, that circle thing with light that is on his head."

I still didn't understand what he was talking about, so I said, "I don't know what you mean."

He sat up and said, "Okay, Mom, you know that thing around his head? It's above his head and it looks like a circle that glows."

It hit me then that he was talking about a halo. Brett has asked me if it's still okay to talk to his Uncle Pat. He says he talks to him at night before he goes to sleep, so if I ever hear him talking a little in his room, that's what he's doing. Then he said he wishes Uncle Pat could just talk back. I told Brett that it certainly was okay that he talks to his Uncle Pat.

I pray daily and always include a request to help me keep my eyes and soul open to signs that God is with me. I pray that I can be reassured that my brother is safe and at peace among the other souls that reside in Heaven.

—*Erin Ryan, Pennsylvania*

I Was Falling into Heaven

We were blessed with three children. However, when our son Brian was murdered in 1989, at the age of nineteen, we had no idea of the impact he would have in the lives of his loved ones many years later. Brian never lived to see his niece and his three nephews.

Approximately ten years later, Brian's youngest nephew Jared, who was then seven years old, had a spiritual experience that saved his life. My daughter-in-law Sheryl's parents were over at her house for Sunday dinner, and Jared's grandfather gave him a Lifesaver candy. Jared being a typically active child jumped up on the couch. When he did this, the Lifesaver went down his throat the wrong way and he was choking. Jared lost consciousness for a few seconds. My son Mike, who is Jared's dad, grabbed him and tried to get Jared to cough up the Lifesaver. Finally, my son was able to dislodge the Lifesaver by getting Jared to cough and spit it up. When Jared came to, he told his parents that he was falling into Heaven and someone who looked just like his daddy pushed him back and told him that it was not his time.

Sheryl looked at Mike and told him that this had to be his brother Brian. She got Brian's graduation picture and showed it to Jared.

"Is this the person who pushed you out of Heaven?"

"Yes, but he wasn't wearing a suit."

"What was he wearing?"

"A red T-shirt and jeans."

That was exactly what Brian was wearing when he was murdered. No one in the family knew that fact except my husband and me.

Until that moment, Jared really had no idea who Brian was. As I mentioned, Jared was born years after Brian was killed. All he knew was that he saw someone who looked like his father. Later Jared went on to tell his parents that he sees Brian all the time now. That Brian wakes him up every morning, goes to school with him, and plays games with him. His mother said that once she walked by Jared's closed bedroom door and heard Jared talking to someone. She opened his door and asked him, "Who are you talking to?"

"Brian."

Jared says he likes his bedroom door shut because that is when Brian comes to see him, and when Sheryl opens the door to check on Jared, he goes away. Jared said sometimes they do not talk and Brian just hangs around with him.

I believe that prayer had a lot to do with this. Jared told his mother that he prays all the time and that he loves God a lot. He is a very spiritual child. Jared has also seen other spirits in the house. He said some were bad, so I told Sheryl to say a prayer to protect Jared. This experience has been very comforting to everyone in the family. It validates to everyone in the family that we have indeed had many ADC's from Brian. Brian has two siblings on earth and between them they have five children. Brian has chosen one child from each of his siblings' families to come to. I also thank God for all the precious ADC's that our family members have received.

    —*Phyllis Hotchkiss, Florida*

      www.angelfire.com/realm/angells/encounters/angelstook.html

The Day My House Caught Fire

It was February 1, 2006, in the wee small hours of the morning. I will never forget it. We lost everything in a terrible fire, and I almost lost my life and the lives of my three boys.

That early morning when the fire was raging, my then five-year-old son Mikey came to my room and frantically shook me to try to wake me up. I woke up to flames all around us. Confused and overcome by smoke, I couldn't get it together enough to lead us out of the house on my own. Flames surrounded us and I couldn't see the way out. Little Mikey kept saying, "This way! This way!" until we were all safely out behind him.

Afterward my son Mikey said to me that my brother Jimmy, who had passed over not long before, was there with us and that he kept saying to Mikey to tell me to come this way with the boys. Jimmy was telling him how to get us out of that fire. Jimmy led us to the door and to safety through my son Mikey. He said my brother even had on his favorite hat!

In spite of my grief, I look back at that day and a smile comes across my face. Our loved ones are there even when we think they're not. Thinking of that black day, I see how far I have come. I thought I'd never pull myself back up from losing everything we had. But I'm still here, and with the help of God, my family at Prayer Wave for

After-Death Communication, and my family here in North Carolina, we made it! I've smoke and fire alarms all around now. I'm still paranoid at night and no open flames are allowed in my house. But I feel protection from Heaven. We know that if it were ever to happen again that we wouldn't be alone.

I love you, Jimmy. Thank you my sweet big brother and thank You, God.

—*Candi Hollifield, North Carolina*

Heavenly Hugs

Back in October 2004, our family suffered a huge tragedy. Our daughter Adrianna was only two and a half years old when she was killed in a car accident. Three months after the tragedy, I was lying down with my then seven-year-old son Andrew and reading a bedtime story to him. While reading the story Andrew said to me, "Mommy, Adrianna hugged me last night. She really did, Mom. I knew it was her."

My eyes immediately filled with tears, and I asked, "How did you know the hug was from your little sister?"

"Well, last night when I was trying to fall asleep, I closed my eyes and felt someone hugging me. I thought it was you or daddy until I opened my eyes and there was no one in the room. I closed my eyes again, and I felt the same feeling, only this time I knew it was Adrianna because she hugged me around my waist like she used to." He paused for a second and said, "She did more than hug me, Mom. I saw her face when I opened my eyes. She looked beautiful. There was so much light in the room and around her face. When I looked at her, she smiled, and then I felt my whole body lifting up in the air." Andrew pointed to his ears and said, "There was a whole bunch of music as my body got higher in the air. Real pretty music."

I asked, "Were you scared?"

Andrew said, "Scared of my sister? No, why would I be scared of my little sister? She looked so happy and I knew I was going to be just as happy being with her."

I had to take a deep breath because my son was so incredibly detailed that I knew he was telling me the truth. I asked, "Then what happened, Andrew?" He said, "She slowly released my body down and said, 'I love you,' and right before my eyes, she disappeared."

—*Rachel, Texas*

Creative Memories

When my daughter Jessica was six years old, she kept dreaming of the same woman every night for a few weeks. Jessica would wake me up very early to tell me about her great dreams of this woman. Months went by and one day Jessica and I were at my mother-in-law's house for a visit. We do Creative Memories projects together, so we were looking at photos for our projects. Jessica was walking by us and suddenly stopped and picked up a photo. She looked at me with wide eyes full of complete wonder. She held up a photo and said, "Mommy, *this* is the woman who has been visiting me in my dreams. Who *is* she?"

It turns out that this woman was my mother-in-law's very own mother who passed at the young age of twenty-nine. Wow!

Sometimes God uses children to remind us that our loved ones live on in Heaven and are still very bonded to us through love.

—*Teri Powell*

I'll Always Be with You

We lived in a small apartment till 2003 when we moved to a larger place. A year after our move, I was sitting down at my computer and going through some family photos. I was looking at one photo in particular of my dad, Roger, when he was in his late twenties. He was in the air force at the time the photo was taken. This was years before diabetes and depression took a major toll on his life. He eventually passed from a brain aneurysm in 1991, when he was only fifty-five. I had been very close to my dad all my life, and his passing was very difficult for me to cope with.

My then seven-year-old son Danté walked into my room when I was looking at this particular air force photo of my dad. I asked Danté if he recognized the man in the photo. I knew he'd seen a photo of my dad in the hallway of our former apartment. In that apartment's photo, my dad had a beard and was singing with his country music band, A Touch of Class, but that's all he knew about my dad.

In reply to my question to my son if he recognized the man in the photo, Danté very nonchalantly answered, "He told me, 'I'll always be with you.'"

I was shocked to the point where my hair stood up on the back of my neck. My dad had died in the summer of 1991, and my son wasn't even born until 1997.

So I asked him what he was talking about. My son said that he had seen my dad in the hallway by the front door of our old apartment last summer. Danté thought that he was a stranger at first because he looked so real, just like anyone else to him. He said that he wasn't afraid of him in the least. Normally, Danté would have been terrified had a stranger been in our apartment.

I asked Danté if he meant that he saw the *photo* of my dad that was on the wall in the hallway. But he said that it wasn't the picture that he was talking about because the man had talked to him. Danté said that when he saw him he had a beard and was wearing a cowboy hat, but he looked younger than he did in the photo on the wall.

Danté also went on to tell me that my dad was in the backseat of our car one night when his mother was driving down a very steep hill to pick me up from work. That hill bothered him because of the steep drop-off on the right side of the road. Like me, Danté has always had a fear of heights. My dad stayed with him until they reached the bottom of the hill, and then he just disappeared. That was very much like something my dad would do.

My son gave me a very powerful gift that day and helped ease so much of my own grief over several of my loved ones who are no longer with us. I discovered that they never left. My little boy proved to me that life and love are forever.

I no longer have any fear of death, whether or not it be tomorrow or fifty years from now. The message is clear. Life transcends death. Can there be a greater gift from the ones we love? I do not think so. I used to get very sad at the thought of both of my parents never living to see their grandchildren. Boy, was I so very wrong. They will always be there for their grandchildren, just as they are for each one of us. I have no doubt whatsoever that what my son saw was a gift from God, and I will be forever grateful to Him for it.

—*Don Winslow*

He's Under the Tree

Greg, my father-in-law, died in September 2007. He was very close to my children, his grandchildren. My then five-year-old son Drew was especially close to his grandfather and always referred to him as Papa T. Drew was very affected by his passing. We did not take Drew to the wake or to the funeral, thinking it might scare him. I often wonder whether that was the right decision, but what is done is done.

Since Greg's passing, Drew has seen him many times. The first sighting was several days after Greg was buried. We took Drew and his older brothers to the cemetery. I believe that Drew thought his grandfather would be there when he got there and was disappointed when he wasn't. Suddenly he cried, "Look, there is Papa T!" as he pointed to the sky. The sky was completely clear, except for an inexplicable part of a rainbow. It was awesome to see. Since then, Drew and the rest of us see that rainbow every time we go to the cemetery. Drew is always the first one to spot it.

Drew also says that he sees Papa T. in the stars. He claims that Papa T. is with his father (his great-grandfather, who Drew has never met), and that they are hugging. This seems to comfort him.

On another occasion, we'd gone to the cemetery with Drew, our other boys, my husband, and my mother-in-law for the Forty-Day Memorial, which is celebrated by the Greek Orthodox religion. While we were all standing at the gravesite, Drew kept insisting that Papa T. wasn't there at the gravesite, and he kept pointing to a spot under a nearby big tree. I finally asked Drew if he saw Papa T. there, and he said, "Yes, I do. He likes it better over there." Then Drew walked over there and stayed under the tree to be with his Papa T. I asked him what Papa T. was wearing, and he perfectly described the suit and shirt that we had buried Greg in, and as I said, he wasn't at the wake or funeral, nor did he see what we had chosen for Greg to wear.

Seven months after Greg's passing with Orthodox Easter approaching, we knew it was going to be a very difficult day for all of us as this was going to be the first one without Greg. A few days before Orthodox Easter, Drew was walking off the soccer field with his daddy. As he was holding my husband's hand, he held out his other hand as if he were holding someone else's hand too. He kept laughing and looking at his empty hand. When my husband asked him what he was laughing about, he said, "Look, Daddy, I'm holding two people's hands, yours and Papa T's!"

A day doesn't go by that Drew doesn't talk about how much he misses his Papa T., but the visions seem to give him comfort. Drew's experiences are helping us heal. I feel blessed that my son has these visions. It is a beautiful gift. He is so lucky. I hope that it never ends.

—*Maureen Thomas, Massachusetts*

I Really Like Sitting in Your Lap!

My dear son, Antal, who was almost eleven years old, died very unexpectedly from an accident. This was a horrible shock to our whole family, and we are still trying to process and recover from the grief of his sudden passing. God and Antal are helping us cope with his death through our children's spiritual experiences.

Eva, my then five-year-old daughter, and her friend were at the house of her friend's grandmother and were watching the movie *The Iron Robot.* Eva said that while watching the movie, Antal came and sat on her lap. She described him as wearing a suit, one bow tie, two neckties, nice shoes, nice pants, nice shirt, and a nice jacket. Eva said, "He laughed out loud and told me he really liked sitting on my lap." She said she saw the TV right through her brother and that Antal watched the whole movie with her.

Eva seems to see Antal with some frequency. Just this past New Year's Eve we were driving to a small party, and on the way there, Eva suddenly said, "Antal's here sitting in the seat next to me! Do you see him?" Later she told my wife that she saw him dancing at the party.

It is comforting to us that Eva can see her brother. She will likely grow up with only a vague memory of her older brother. If she sees him frequently, that may not happen, and we certainly want to encourage her to be open to that kind of comforting spiritual experience. Her visions of him seem to come unbidden, and since she is so spontaneous in what she says, there is no reason for us to doubt her.

—*Endre Balogh, California*
www.endresphotos.com

Brian and Grampy Together Again

In October 2005 my husband Duane was diagnosed with stage 3 non-small cell lung cancer. The prognosis was bleak and Duane was basically preparing himself and our whole family for his death. We had been married for forty-two years, and this news was devastating to me.

In February I called hospice to provide care in our home for Duane. My son Michael, his wife Sheryl, and their two children

Jared, eight, and Samantha, fourteen, at the time, came to my house to see Duane. He was in a hospital bed in our living room, and Mike figured that this would be the last time that the kids would be seeing their grandfather alive. Mike and Sheryl had prepared them, telling them that Grampy was very sick and would soon be in Heaven with God. They had a nice visit with Duane, even though at times he was sleeping due to the medication. When it came time to say good-bye, Mike, Sheryl, Samantha, and Jared took turns going to his bedside kissing him and hugging him and telling him that they loved him.

About five minutes after they left, I got a phone call. It was my daughter-in-law Sheryl. I could tell that she was crying, and I could hear some sniffling in the background. She said that when they got into the car, Samantha and Jared were in the backseat, and she suddenly heard Samantha crying. Sheryl turned around and asked her what was wrong. Samantha explained that her brother Jared just told her that when they were all hugging and kissing Grampy, he saw his Uncle Brian sitting in a chair crying. (Brian was our son who was murdered in 1989 at the age of nineteen.) Sheryl put Jared on the phone, and he told me all that he saw.

Jared had been seeing dead people for a quite a long time, so we believed him. Jared has been seeing and talking to his Uncle Brian for at least three years. However, Jared was crying and upset because this was the only time he had ever seen his Uncle Brian crying. I told him Uncle Brian knew that Grampy (Brian's dad) was going to be dying soon and going to Heaven. Even though Uncle Brian and Grampy were going to be happy to see each other, his Uncle Brian was crying and sad because we were all so sad. I told Jared it was all right to cry and we would all be sad when Grampy died. But I said Grampy would be really happy to be in Heaven with God and his son Brian, and he wouldn't want us to be sad all the time.

Duane went to be with the Lord a week and a half later on March 7, 2006. Since his passing, Jared has told me that he sees Grampy and Uncle Brian all the time in his house. He talks to Brian, but that

Grampy hasn't talked to him as yet, but when Grampy does talk to him, Jared told me that he'd let me know.

It is comforting for everyone in our family when any one of us gets an ADC. We always share them with each other, and we are never afraid to talk about them. Prayer also plays a big part in our lives. I truly believe that with God in your life, you can get through anything. I have gotten through the murder of my son and the passing of my husband of forty-two years. I have been praying that the Holy Spirit shines on my family and me so that we can be happy knowing that my husband Duane is with his son Brian, his mother, his father, and his sister. And most of all, I pray that he is with God. Since praying that, I have peace in my heart and do not have too many moments of sadness.

—*Phyllis Hotchkiss, Florida*
duane-hotchkiss.memory-of.com/About.aspx

Seven Little Puppies

I have a wonderful little granddaughter named Jessica Anne. Before our twenty-three-year-old son Ashley went on Home to Heaven, he and Jessica Anne had a unique and special bond, unlike any I have ever seen. I believe they are kindred souls. Our son adored her. She was only a little over two years old when her uncle Ashley died.

Jessica Anne has talked about Ashley visiting her in dreams after he passed over. On more than one occasion, Jessica Anne has come out of her bedroom in the morning and shared stories of her dreams about her Uncle Ashley. In her dreams they have participated in fun activities together. They have gone swimming, he has pushed her swing for her, and they have even gone on picnics together. These dreams have been so vivid that one could almost watch them come alive as she was speaking about them to us.

On July 6, 2007, when Jessica Anne was eight years old, she woke up and told her mother that she had another dream in which her

Uncle Ashley visited her. Jessica Anne said that Ashley told her that her mother's dog Roxie was going to have her puppies the very next day on July 7, 2007. He told her that there would be seven of them. She said that Ashley told her that he would be looking out for her and would visit again soon.

Sure enough the next evening Roxie gave birth to seven little puppies. And just think, we knew beforehand exactly when they were going to be born because of Ashley's dream visit to Jessica Anne.

For Jessica Anne, these visits are a gift from Heaven, and she will tell anyone, who will listen, that God loves us enough that He sends our loved ones to us in dreams sometimes. I think she has a good start in life with an attitude like that about God's love.

—*Donna Bowman, Florida*

Daddy Is Standing Beside You

As far back as I can remember, my daughter Tiyanna has always been different from my other children in that she senses and knows things she could not have possibly known about on her own. I used to think she had lots of imaginary friends, but now when I look back, I believe these were really spirits communicating with her.

For instance, her Grandmother Whyard, my husband's mother, died when my husband was only three years old. Grandmother Whyard was a taboo topic we did not talk about in our house, so my children did not know about her. Yet Tiyanna used to tell us that her grandma would kiss her good-night. She said that one time she got up to go to the bathroom and that she saw this pretty woman in the hallway. The woman said to her, "Tiyanna, it's okay. I'm your grandma and I love you. I'll always watch over you."

At first I thought, yeah, right, she must have been sleepwalking. But then I became curious and asked Tiyanna what the woman looked like. I pulled out some photo albums that Tiyanna has never seen. They were hidden away because my husband never liked talking about his mother, and I did not want to distress him. Tiyanna picked Grandmother Whyard's picture out of the album!

I wrote this story sixteen months after I lost my beloved husband of fifteen years. Well, things have been so awfully hard, especially taking care of our five little ones, who are solely dependent on me. This responsibility added a lot of stress on top of their losing their dad. How do you get over losing that person you loved so much? I never thought I would. I am better these days, due to my daughter's gift.

Before my husband passed, he had promised us that he would make sure we would all be happy and okay. I believe he has kept his promise by the things that have happened to my daughter Tiyanna who is now 9 years old.

Tiyanna often says, "Mommy, Daddy is standing beside you, and he wants you to know it's gonna be okay." Tiyanna is so full of life and misses him so much. He was her best friend. She says he comes at night sometimes and kisses her sisters and her good-night.

Now looking back on more of the inexplicable things Tiyanna has done or said, I absolutely believe it's true that she can see and hear her daddy and others. My husband did promise he would always be here with her, no matter where he was, and that he would only be a whisper away. I believe Tiyanna's gift is a gift from God to help comfort us, and that my husband *is* only a whisper away.

—*Tammy Whyard*

Dancing the Hula

We were on our way to church one day when my then six-year-old daughter, who was sitting in the backseat of the car, asked, "How did my Nana die?"

"Cancer," I said.

"If Nana had cancer, why did she have her hair?" she asked.

"The medicine is what causes people to lose their hair, and Nana was too sick to get the medicine," I said.

When we got to church, as we were exiting the car, she walked up to me smiling and very calmly said, "Nana was just sitting next to me in the backseat." She explained in a child's vocabulary basically that her Nana had nudged her to move over to make room for her. Then my daughter described more about what she saw. "It was her whole body, head, face, arms, and legs. She was doing the Hula!"

I told her that she was very lucky to have had Nana come to visit her like that.

Later that evening, I wanted to know more about my mother's visit. I asked my daughter if she was asking questions about Nana's hair because Nana was sitting next to her, and she replied, "Yes." I think my daughter may still have been trying to figure out why her Nana had her hair even though she knew that some people with cancer lost their hair.

She also told me that Nana looked very pretty with makeup and that she was wearing a black-and-white skirt and a white shirt. She mentioned that it was the same outfit she was wearing at her funeral mass. Now my daughter had gone to the funeral mass, but she had never actually viewed my mother's body at the mass! Because there was no logical explanation as to how my daughter would know what her Nana was wearing at the mass, I asked my daughter if she also *saw* Nana at the funeral mass. She replied, "Yes." So this explains how my daughter knew what my mother wore at her funeral mass because my mother had appeared to her there.

Since the day my mother died, my daughter has been telling me that Nana is in Heaven dancing. Maybe she really is.

—*Karen, Connecticut*

Christmas Mass with Daddy

When my daughter Britney was eight years old, she saw her deceased father at her Catholic school's Christmas Mass that year. This was the first Christmas since he passed over just seven weeks earlier from lung cancer and septic shock.

After the sermon about the birth of Jesus and before Holy Communion was distributed, Britney noticed her father in a corner of the church. He was standing in close proximity to the priest. He looked at Britney and waved with his right hand in a half-bent, cupping formation.

Britney said he was wearing a white robe and a big white smile to match. He also looked to be in perfect health and looked very good. Britney whispered, "Hello," to her dad, and then the image of her dad went poof.

In Britney's nightly prayers, she had been asking God for a peaceful communication from her father. This was very comforting to Britney and made her very happy. She felt God had answered her prayers.

—*Amy C., New Jersey*

Why Is He Wearing a Dress?

My precious brother tragically died from being shot in the head. This was devastating to us. Soon after his passing, something really unexplainable happened. We were visiting my sister at her house when my six-year-old son Kevin came running toward me very excitedly. I asked him what was wrong. He said that his uncle, my brother, was in the other room looking at my other young son, Freddy.

Kevin then asked me why my brother was wearing a dress—he said he had on a white dress. I realized that the white dress my brother was wearing must have been his new heavenly garment to show us that he was indeed in Heaven and not to worry about him.

One night, three years later, we were getting ready to eat dinner when my son Kevin, who was then nine years old, suddenly jumped up and hugged me and started to cry. I didn't understand what could possibly be wrong. I asked him what was going on? He said, "It's my uncle. He is right there looking at me!" And he pointed to near the dining room table, which was only a few feet away from us.

I could not see anything myself though. But my very startled and frightened son saw my brother's spirit there for at least two minutes until I finally asked Kevin to ask my brother please to leave. After my son asked him to leave, my brother left immediately. I am sure he did not want to frighten us, but rather he was coming to visit us to let us know that he still watched over us. But the experience startled both my son and me. I think because of my son's reaction, I was a little frightened too. We just weren't expecting this. It had been three years (at the time) since my brother's last spiritual visit, and we were not too familiar with this type of spiritual phenomenon.

However, when I think back, ever since my son Kevin could talk, he would often tell me that there were people in the mirrors. Since I didn't know back then that children could often see and hear spirits, even in mirrors, I told him that this was just his imagination. Now I believe him wholeheartedly, and I am no longer frightened by these loving spiritual appearances because I have come to understand them.

—Isabel Calderon

Grandpa's Here

We have always been a close-knit family. My husband always referred to us—my daughter, my granddaughter, and me—as "my girls." We owned a small gourmet bakery, which was run by my husband and my daughter. When our granddaughter was born, she would spend the day with her mother and her grandfather at the bakery. Having an infant there was a challenge, but my husband and my daughter stepped up, and my husband loved every minute of it. As a toddler our granddaughter would welcome the customers, and after their purchases, she would escort them to the door, thanking them for their business. My husband, my daughter, and our grand-daughter made quite a team at our bakery.

After we closed the business, my husband (Grandpa) was re-cruited to pick up our granddaughter from preschool and then watch her until her mother came home from work. They were bud-dies! They laughed and cried together. They would go out for lunch and for ice cream. Grandpa loved to tickle and tease her.

My husband's illness was sudden and unexpected. We never left his side. His illness and death left us in deep and utter despair. I lost my best friend, my high school sweetheart, the love of my life, and my heart's inspiration. My daughter lost a father who loved her with all his heart. My granddaughter lost her buddy. We were in the dark-est days of our lives, and yet in our hearts, we felt that we were still his girls.

A few days after the funeral, I received a call from my daughter. Her voice sounded nervous and she spoke quickly. She told me about how they had just gotten home. She went upstairs and her daughter stayed downstairs in the family room. Out of the blue her daughter called out to her, "Grandpa's here." My daughter immedi-ately went downstairs to see what she was talking about. No one was there—that she could see.

Her then five-year-old daughter explained that Grandpa was sit-ting where he always sat and that he smiled at her. She wasn't upset and she went back to playing after she explained to her mother what had happened. My daughter didn't want to talk about it with me at any length, and I could tell she was upset about it. However, my granddaughter's experience brought me a great deal of comfort. Al-though, I'll admit that I wished that I'd had seen him too!

Several weeks after that, we were on my driveway, and my daugh-ter and granddaughter were about to get into their car to go home when a butterfly started circling us. We were all taken by how beau-tiful the butterfly looked in the sunlight. Suddenly I found myself putting my hand up into the air and telling my granddaughter that the butterfly was going to land on my hand. To my amazement, it did. I don't know why I said or did that. I've never had a butterfly land on my hand by command! It stayed on my hand for the longest time as if it belonged to me. Then it left. Seconds later it was back, and once again it landed on my hand. We were all amazed, and I know in my heart it was my husband letting his girls know that he was still around watching over us and that he was all right. We were still his girls.

It has been almost three years since my husband's death. Since then I have had numerous contacts with him, all of which have helped to heal my broken heart. I believe that the love that we share never ends and that this love allows us to stay connected beyond the veil.

—*Paula M. Ezop, Illinois*

Pop-pop Helps Me Surf

When my little granddaughter Sophie was three years old, my husband passed on. Sophie now lives by the beach with my son and daughter-in-law. She is a very active little girl, like her daddy, and loves surfing, skateboarding, snowboarding, and other activities on wheels!

One day last summer, when Sophie was seven years old, my son was working with her to strengthen her surfing skills. He was amazed at how this petite girly girl seemed to have no fear when riding on the surfboard. So he asked her if she was ever afraid when she was surfing. She answered very quickly, "No, because Pop-pop helps me!"

Astounded by this answer my son asked a few more questions. She told him that Pop-pop helps her with lots of things, and that when she was little, she would see Pop-pop at Granny's (my) house. My son stopped asking questions at this point as he didn't want to cause her to question the relationship she seemed to have with her Pop-pop.

When my son relayed this conversation to me, I remembered a couple of times when Sophie was four and five years old and they were visiting me after my husband passed that she would come and tell me she saw someone in my bedroom.

I am so happy that my granddaughter is able to be comforted and continues to know her grandfather!

—*Sandi Riley, New Jersey*

Swimming with My Brother

My big brother Frankie, died on May 20, 2004, a few days before he was to give his Fairfield University valedictorian speech to his graduating class. He had been attending a spring formal dance with his girlfriend Anna in Newport, Rhode Island, and he was walking back to his hotel when he was confronted by a group of students on a pub crawl. They pushed him backward just as a bus was rounding the corner, and the bus ran over Frankie.

I miss him a lot. We were the best of friends and loved playing ball and riding bikes together. Every night since Frankie was killed, I say the "Angel of God" prayer so that he has a great new life and that someday we will be together again.

On Saturday, September 3, 2005, when I was nine years old, I had a wonderful dream in which Frankie came and visited me. In my dream, I was playing in the woods behind my house with my best friend Jake. It was nighttime and we had flashlights. As we walked into the side yard, I looked over toward the pool and saw a face in the deep end. I then shined my flashlight over there and saw that it was my brother Frankie staring back at me!

I walked over toward the pool with Jake, and as I reached the cement, my brother Frankie swam just under the surface toward the swimout (access out of a pool's deep end). As I reached the swimout, he was floating on the water, and I screamed with joy, "Frankie!" I was so excited and happy to see him again! I jumped into his arms to give him a big hug and just went right through him. I immediately woke up from my dream.

I was so excited about Frankie's visit that I just had to tell someone. I came downstairs and told my mom that I needed to talk with her in private. I told her about my incredible dream visit from Frankie. She started to cry. She said that it was amazing and that her tears were tears of joy because she had been waiting for a visit from Frankie as well. This experience really helped me know that my big brother will still come to visit and play with me.

—*Patrick Marx, Pennsylvania*
www.francisjmarxv.com

The Birthday Celebration

My daughter began seeing "people" in our house when she was about three years old. It started with her saying she had seen someone walking from one room to another. I would go with her to look in the rooms to verify that no one else was there, so she could continue to play safely in the room.

When she was five years old she was better able to explain the things she saw. She told me that she saw my brother Michael who was killed almost ten years ago. She saw a small boy with him at times. She also saw many other people but at that time she was unaware of who they were. Seeing strangers at times was scary when she was so young, and I don't think the people she saw were aware of her age. Knowing that she saw my brother though was a great comfort to my parents and me.

Last week she let us know that Michael was sad about his birthday that was coming up in two weeks. She did not know his birthday was approaching when she said this to us. You see, before she was born, we celebrated Michael's birthday yearly, even though he had passed, but as time went by we stopped this practice. So finding out that this was important to him has changed our minds about celebrating his birthday.

For other parents out there who have children who are blessed with this gift, I can only say believe in your children and give them the understanding that someone with their gifts needs and deserves. Even if you don't understand what they are going through, find someone who does.

—*Kristy Lagunas, Arizona*

The Woman and the Car Ride

One day I was driving home in my car with my then five-year-old son Kyle sitting alone in the back in his car seat when I heard him having a one-sided conversation with someone else. I tried readjusting my rearview mirror to see whom he was talking to, but I didn't see anyone else.

I asked him whom he was talking to, and he said, "The woman next to me."

I asked a few more questions along the lines of "Is she kind?" "Is she scary?" "Do you feel safe?" All of Kyle's answers indicated that he didn't mind her being there.

Because I can also feel, hear, and speak to spirits myself, and I did not feel any malice in the car with us, I let them have their conversation, which seemed to go very nicely. Their conversation had to do with everyday things that he did and with him liking the car ride.

—*Melody, Pennsylvania*

Shhhh

My granddaughter Monica has mentioned seeing her Angel Uncle Louie, my son, many times in her young life. Before she began school, when her mind was so free and open, she would often speak of Louie visiting her. My son Louie passed over when Monica was about one and a half years old.

One special time was on her fifth birthday. It was a beautiful, warm, and sunny day on the twenty-first of October when I arrived early to my daughter Tiffany's house to help her set up for Monica's birthday party. My daughter Tiffany had twenty-four shiny-colored Mylar helium balloons outside with all Dora The Explorer decorations for Monica's party.

Monica was running around the outside of the house by herself and kept hiding in the shrubs. I asked her, "What the heck are you doing?"

She yelled back that Uncle Louie was playing hide-and-seek with her.

I said, "Well that's great. What does he look like?"

She replied, "He's a big, giant uncle, and he likes to giggle a lot! and he was saying 'Shhhhhh.'" Monica pointed to her mouth and said he had his finger to his mouth, like when someone does when they want you to keep a secret. Monica announced that he was staying for the party and then going back to Heaven. Since Louie was six feet three inches tall, weighed 270 pounds, and was also the clown in the family, I knew she was really talking to my son. This gave my heart so much joy knowing he was actually there celebrating with us.

We had a great day with games, face painting, and lots of presents. It was really such a sweet and wonderful day. Louie's present was his actual presence there! His love reached out to all of us that day. We took lots of photos to remember the occasion.

When the pictures from the party were developed, they showed the most beautifully colored circle orbs, which were the same colors as the balloons! Yet, the pictures were taken away from where the balloons were hanging, so they did not get captured in these photos. There is no earthly explanation for those colored orbs showing up in the photos. I believe my son Louie was showing his spiritual presence in these photos as further proof he was there for Monica's birthday party. I know Louie had a great time being there too. I believe, as does the rest of my family, that all our loved ones are near us, watching over.

—Pattyann Schmidt, Pennsylvania

The Policeman's Teddy Bear

My son Matthew, who happens to have Down syndrome, seems to have a direct connection with my beloved father, who sadly passed very unexpectedly from a massive heart attack at the young age of fifty-three. My son never had the pleasure of meeting my precious father on earth because he was born many years later.

There have been quite a number of times when out of the blue Matthew will give me a message from my dad. What usually transpires right before my son gives me a message is that he acts as if he were shocked by a slight jolt of electricity. When I notice this happening to Matthew, I always ask him what's going on. He'll say something like, "It's Poppy and he wants me to tell you he loves you" or "He wants you to be happy."

The most incredible experience happened one night while I was sitting on the couch in the family room. I was reading a novel about a man in a hospital room who suddenly went into cardiac arrest and died. The nurse in the story was very upset because this man had reminded her so much of her own father, a police officer, who died the same way. The story continued with the man in the other bed in this semiprivate room asking the distraught nurse why there was a police officer in the room. The nurse said, "There's no police officer in the room." He insisted that there was and that the police officer was standing right behind her holding a teddy bear. The nurse was stunned, because "Teddy Bear" was the nickname her policeman dad used to call her.

Well, I got the goose bumps as I was reading this part of the story because of the similarity of both of our dads' deaths and the coincidence of the spirit of her dad being in the room with her while she was thinking about him. At that moment, my then five-year-old son Matthew, a special needs child, walked into the family room. He was trying to get my attention by exclaiming, "Mommy! Mommy!"

I told him to wait just a moment so I could finish the last few lines of that chapter. Then I asked, "What's the matter, Matthew?"

He said, "It's Poppy. He wants me to give you a big hug and tell you that he loves you!"

I was astonished! My husband was also sitting on the couch reading, and I said, "You have *got* to read this." I handed him the book and showed him what I had just finished reading. I then mentioned how uncanny the timing was of Matthew's message from my dad with the similarity of the story.

My husband was astonished too. We both agreed that we would never ever doubt that my son's messages were really from my father. I am so grateful that my father has found a way to communicate his love for me through my son. So often the messages come just when I need them the most.

—*Mary Beaury Paladino, Pennsylvania*

Uncle Eric Heard My Plea

At the time my daughter Blaire was in first grade, we had a very close friend of the family, her Uncle Eric, who was like a second father to her. Eric would come over and spend quality time with her, take her places, buy her gifts, and so on. They really loved each other.

Eric took ill and passed away at the very young age of forty-two. Needless to say, Blaire was devastated, as was the whole family. The day after he passed, she was extremely nervous, crying, and trying to come to terms with his death since this was her first experience losing someone very close to her. I realized that if her Uncle Eric knew she was in turmoil over him, he would make it right. So I asked him to!

That evening, Blaire went to bed grieving deeply, and the next morning she woke up a new person. She was calm and more like herself. I asked her if she was all right, and she said that she saw Uncle Eric last night. He was all dressed up in a suit and tie, and she described his clothing in detail. He told her not to worry because he wasn't sick anymore and he was fine. He also told her to take care of her "Momma," which is how he always referred to me. After her contact with her Uncle Eric, although she missed him dearly, she was able to deal with his death.

I am so thankful that her Uncle Eric heard my plea for help and came and visited her from Heaven to ease her grief.

—*Maryanne*

Jesus and Heaven

My husband passed in 2007 from lung cancer and septic shock. He always claimed he was six feet tall, but was really five feet eleven inches tall. Our daughter Britney was very close to him and still misses him dearly. Britney, who is now nine years old has seen him on a number of occasions since his passing.

Britney has told me that while awake in bed, a spirit who is about six feet tall comes to her. When the spirit is here, sometimes she will feel little kisses on her cheeks or feelings of her head being rubbed. The spirit is almost invisible and wears a white robe. Sometimes he speaks softly, and says "Hello." She has the distinct impression that this spirit is her daddy.

Once Britney had a dream about her dad. In this dream, Britney had a butterfly net and was walking along a trail happily catching butterflies. A spirit came by on the trail. Britney knew that this was the same spirit who had rubbed her head when she was lying awake in bed—her daddy. The spirit said, "Hi." Then Britney asked him if he wanted to catch butterflies with her. The spirit told Britney that he did, but he didn't have a net. Britney, who happened to have two nets gave him one, and they had fun catching butterflies together.

Another time Britney had an extra special dream. It was a vision of Heaven. She saw someone whom she believed to be Jesus. She described Him as having long hair and wearing a white robe and sandals. In this heavenly place, Britney also saw waterfalls and buffet tables filled with food. She saw her daddy and Jesus standing together talking, and she remembers that she heard them talking about walking along the waterfalls.

Recently, Britney has surprised me by telling me that she has seen Jesus sitting on my bed and that Jesus has long brown hair. I am always in awe of the supernatural experiences that Britney has had. They have helped to bring us enormous joy and peace and have strengthened our belief that our loved ones who are in Heaven still continue to be a part of our lives.

—*Amy C., New Jersey*

I Just Saw Grandpop

My father died of lung cancer three months before my wedding. It was a very difficult time for us. Then my mother was diagnosed with breast cancer one month after I was married. I wanted to get pregnant quickly because I was afraid that I was going to lose my mother, and I wanted her to see her first grandchild, something my father missed out on. Six months after I was married, I became pregnant with my baby, Danielle.

When my daughter, Danielle, was born, she was the bright light in our family. She helped my mom get through her cancer and thankfully she beat it. The entire time I kept my father's memory alive for Danielle and spoke of him often. She always seemed to miss him and felt the loss of her grandfather that she had never known. I always told her to look for signs because I received them often, such as cigar smoke.

I believe the spirit world can communicate with us, and my daughter was fortunate enough not only to get a sign but also to see my dad (her grandfather) twice—once when she was eight years old and another time when she was nine years old.

The first time he visited her, when she was eight years old, she woke me and told me that she had seen her grandfather. She described what he looked like and explained the entire experience to me.

"Mom, I just saw Grandpop."

I groggily opened my eyes and said, "Where is he?" thinking it was my father-in-law who was still alive.

"Mom I just saw Grandpop, the one in Heaven!" she said again.

"Okay, Danielle, go back to sleep," I replied, dismissing what she had said. I closed my eyes again and thought about what I had just heard. Could she have really seen my father? I called her to come back into my room again to find out if she was talking about my father, and she was.

I asked Danielle, who is now a young adult, to share her recollections in more detail. She agreed to tell her story reluctantly because she had only written about a deceased family member once when on a spiritual retreat called Kairos. Here is what she told me:

"I was about eight years old when I first saw my grandfather. As a child I suffered from insomnia slightly, so if I did drift off to sleep, it wasn't for long. It was about eleven-thirty at night when I happened to look up at my doorway. Normally I was afraid of the slightest sound when I was alone in my bed, but this was different. In the doorway was a man ready to say good-night and check in on his granddaughter. I was trying to comprehend who I was seeing, but all I knew was that I wasn't afraid. I saw a man about fifty, with dark olive skin, balding with his belly showing through this thin V-necked T-shirt. His jeans were slightly distressed from wear and tear and the belt that held them up was under his stomach. His appearance was like an apparition, slightly transparent, and the whole episode probably lasted about two seconds. I just knew this was my grandfather. Instead of lying in my bed screaming with the covers over my head,

I went downstairs to tell my mother. I remember the tears in her eyes and the smile on her face.

"About a year later, I was playing at my other grandmother's house. Someone walked into the house across the living room and into the kitchen. I looked up and said, "Hello," and I got a "Hi" back. Everything had happened so quickly. I walked into the other room where my grandmother was ironing, and I said, "Is anyone here?" She looked at me quite puzzled, and I said, "I just saw my grandpop walk through the house. Didn't you hear us talking?" But she hadn't. The communication was telepathic, something that I later found out often occurs with spirits.

"This time he was wearing a light blue shirt and jeans. He had the same appearance as last time, but instead it was during the daytime, which is usually the opposite. Most people talk about seeing spirits at nighttime.

"These visions are ingrained in my brain, etched into my memory. I may forget my fifth Christmas or my sixteenth birthday, but these images burn happily in my mind. Sadly, I have not seen him since. Maybe, hopefully soon, when I open a door or look out a window, I will be pleasantly surprised."

—*Danielle and Lori, Pennsylvania*

Surrounded by Light

My grandson Ethan has always been curious about his relatives, those here and those who have passed. I have pictures in my living room of all of them. Since about the age of three, Ethan has told us of incidents about afterlife visits with his grandmother and grandfather. These descriptions and information were things he could not possibly have known on his own.

One day when Ethan was seven years old, Ethan's mother came to me and told me that just a few days before, Ethan had told her about a recent afterlife visit from his great-grandmother Germaine Marguerite Sire Moone. In this visit, Germaine told him that she would always protect him and would be there to watch over him. Ethan described her as being surrounded by a white light, and she was wearing a gown of blue and white. Just the top half of her body was visible to him. From Ethan's description she looked the same age as she did when she passed away because she had snow-white hair. The visit was very brief, and then she disappeared. Ethan said his great-grandmother appeared to him in his bedroom. At the time he was alone and sitting on the floor, playing with his things.

Germaine was a very petite woman, only five feet tall, but in life she was the matriarch of our family and raised three sons and one daughter. Germaine was also a French teacher, and she just loved children. She was the warmest and lovingest person anyone could ever meet. It does not surprise me that she would appear out of love and affection for her great-grandson Ethan, especially since she knows Ethan has the ability to see spirits very easily. What a beautiful and tender way to show him that she is forever a part of his life. This visit meant a lot to all of us.

—*Monique Moore, Florida*

Tommy's Head

Tommy is my son. On August 24, 1997, at the young age of fifteen, he was killed instantly by a local drunk driver, who never showed any remorse. I cannot begin to describe the pain that my family and I suffered over the unexpected and sudden loss of Tommy.

My dear grandson Gabriel never met his Uncle Tommy as he wasn't born until two years later. When Gabriel was only five years old, he had an incredible spiritual experience concerning my son Tommy.

It was a hot summer day, and Gabriel's mother was trying to wake him up for school. While she was calling to him, Gabriel simultaneously felt a cold breeze and went to grab the blue and white plaid blankets on the bed to cover himself up. Gabriel looked at the blankets that he was about to grab and saw that the blankets were lying in the shape of a T-shirt, and on top of the T-shirt-shaped blankets was my son Tommy's head.

Gabriel was not afraid and was so excited to see his Uncle Tommy that he couldn't wait to tell his mother and me all about it. I asked, "Oh, wow! You really saw Tommy?"

And Gabriel said in the most unshakeable and adamant way, "Yes, I saw him!"

After missing my son so much, to learn that he was still a part of our lives was so comforting to know. I loved the fact that Tommy wanted his little nephew finally to "meet" him.

—*Deborah Mathewsk, California*
atouchofheart-poetry.webs.com

Sometimes Papa Is Here

My husband's name was Rodney. He was extremely close to our children and grandchildren. Jaylan, our then six-year-old grandson, always said Papa was his best friend.

My husband passed unexpectedly on December 20, 2007, at the age of forty-seven. Rodney was the picture of health, very fit and active. That morning he woke me up and said his chest hurt and that his arms were numb.

I was frantic and said, "We have to go to the hospital immediately." He said, "Maybe it's just indigestion!"

I said, "No way! We're going!" I ran downstairs to get the car keys and then heard him yell my name. I raced back upstairs, and thankfully our son was upstairs and was able to catch him just as he fell. Our then seventeen-year-old daughter, who was a lifeguard, and I did CPR on him till the ambulance arrived. The staff at the hospital continued to work on him, but he was already gone.

Our oldest daughter, Ryanne, and her children lived with us. Rodney was like a father figure to our grandchildren as their father floated in and out of their lives. It was about a month after Rodney's passing that the grandchildren started telling us they were seeing Papa. One of the first times my grandson Jaylan saw him, Jaylan was playing on the living room floor. Suddenly, he stopped and looked up and said, "Papa is here. Look, he's standing right there! Papa is smiling at me! Papa says he loves me."

Another time Jaylan was in the living room watching TV. He looked toward the dining room and said that he saw Papa holding Spike, our toy Pomeranian, who died a couple of years before Rodney. He said Rodney was sitting in the computer chair. Rodney has also come to Jaylan in his dreams.

Another time Mya, our then three-year-old granddaughter, and I were sitting on the couch in the living room. She said, "Grandma, there's Papa!" She was pointing to the middle of the living room. A couple of minutes later she said, "Papa is gone now." My granddaughter has also said on another occasion, "Grandma, sometimes Papa isn't in Heaven, sometimes he's here."

The morning before he died, Rodney said to me, out of the blue, "I'll never leave you, honey." He hasn't. Other family members and I have also had ADCs with Rodney. It's very comforting to know he still checks in on us! I'm still madly in love with him. Our kids used to say we were like two teenagers in love. We were always holding hands and kissing. Rodney was and is the love of my life.

—*Patty McClung, Michigan*

Your Mom Is an Angel

My grandbaby Judie seems to have the same gift as I do. Growing up, I didn't fully understand that I was communicating with spirits until I reached adulthood. People didn't talk about those things back then or have the awareness that they do now. I'm so happy there's more understanding about spiritual communications nowadays.

Here's a spiritual visitation that happened to my grandbaby Judie just a couple of months ago when she was six years old.

Little Judie was downstairs playing in the den at the time. My daughter and I were upstairs in her bedroom. We heard little Judie talking to someone. Since the three of us were the only ones in the house at the time, I turned and asked my daughter, "Who is Judie talking to?"

"I told you, Mom, she does that a lot."

Well upon hearing this one-sided conversation coming from little Judie downstairs, I, of course, was extremely curious, and I had to sneak down the stairs to listen in more closely. When I got there, I heard little Judie say, "I love you too. My mom mom misses you."

How cool is that? That's all I heard her say. Nothing else, and she was all alone.

I showed myself to her and said, "Baby, who were you talking to?"

"Your mom, she comes and sees me a lot."

Well, my eyes started to well up with tears. Just to know that my mother visits little Judie and is around a lot really made me feel very emotional and long to see her again. My little grandbaby comforted me by saying, "Don't cry, Mom Mom. Your mom is an angel and she is beautiful. You will see her again!"

Freaked me out! She sounded like an old soul instead of a little girl.

Oh, normally my granddaughter will not want to stay in the den by herself unless someone is in there with her. So the times that she is in there alone and feeling secure, my daughter will remark that Mom Mom must be in there playing with her. My daughter called my mother Mom Mom too.

I think that my little Judie is going to continue to be a lot like me. She sees and talks to spirits often and does not show any fear of them. To her it must just seem like a real live person she is talking to. I remember that is the way I felt as a child. I am so thankful that she has this gift and can let us know when my mother is around. This really warms my heart.

—*Judie Ziegler Alliano, New Jersey*

Grampy Joe's Cake

I never met my husband's grandfather, Grampy Joe, since he died before I met my husband. I felt that since it was possible that he was also watching over our daughter Kirsten, we would honor him with a birthday cake for his birthday. So I made one the morning of what would have been his birthday.

That evening my husband was a little late getting home from work, and we ate dinner later than usual, around 6:30 P.M. I was cleaning up and had a small job to do in the office before I was going to serve the cake. But the entire time I was in the office trying to focus, I kept thinking it was time to serve the cake, as if a voice in my head were saying, "Let's go. Come on. Light the candles!" This was actually getting so annoying and distracting that I couldn't think straight. Just when I felt I was going to lose my mind, my daughter Kirsten came in and said to me, "Mommy, I think Grampy Joe is getting impatient. He wants to have his cake. He is waiting for us to sing."

I thought, "My daughter, this little five-year-old girl, has heard from Grampy Joe! I am not crazy!" I hugged her and said, "Then let's go get Grampy Joe's candles lit and have some cake!"

I called in my husband and said, "I am sorry, but Grampy Joe is getting impatient and wants us to celebrate now!" My husband laughed. Then I explained what happened to both Kirsten and me.

My husband chuckled and said, "He used to do that with my grandmother and with us all the time. Just couldn't wait to have his cake and for all of us to sing to him. Grampy Joe was like a little kid on his birthday; he just couldn't wait!"

I never met the man, but I felt that I had to make a cake for his birthday that day. That's the only time I ever did make him a cake. Haven't before or since. Maybe that's why he was so excited and antsy. He just wanted to celebrate with us I guess. It was pretty funny.

—*Karen Janney, New Jersey*

The Cards Showed Daddy's Life

My husband Michael died on March 26, 2007, after a two-year battle with leukemia and lymphoma. I am a firm believer in messages from Heaven. Ever since my husband's passing, he has been sending my daughter and me messages. These have been incredible experiences for us.

My daughter Michaela had a visit from my husband on the morning of April 4, 2008. She was seven years old at the time. She woke up screaming and crying and wanting her daddy.

Here's the visit that happened to Michaela. "Daddy flew up to the ceiling and then cards appeared. He touched the cards. The cards showed Daddy's life. Then I saw Daddy's funeral. The last card had nothing on it because that's when he died; then Daddy disappeared."

Michaela described what he was wearing. He was wearing his favorite blue and white striped shirt, black pants, no glasses, and a mustache. Michael was a cancer patient, so the mustache meant he was showing himself looking healthy before his diagnosis in May 2005. At the time of the dream, we were leaving that day to spend the weekend at Great Wolfe Lodge. I believed Michael was wishing her a fun trip. She really screamed so much that I figured she scared him away! We wrote the dream down, she signed it, and we dated it.

A good friend interpreted the dream and said that Michael was trying to teach Michaela about his life and to tell her where he was now. He was trying to show her what Heaven was like with the last card. He tried to let her know that he was okay.

Michael came back again to visit on the morning of July 12, 2008. As it turns out, he visited right before another trip we were taking. We were going to be driving from New Jersey to the Outer Banks of North Carolina. I woke my daughter up at 6:25 A.M. so that we could get an early start. Michaela said she was dreaming about Daddy right at the time I woke her up. She said he had a mustache and was wearing glasses.

Michael loved the beach and especially the Outer Banks! So it seems so timely that he would come to be with her right before another trip! I believe he wanted us to know that he was aware of our plans and was happy for us. These visits to my daughter have been so comforting for all of us. I cherish them.

—*Lauren Ryan, New Jersey*

Granddad Has Powers

My husband died under tragic circumstances in August 2006. Within days, one of our grandsons began conversing with him. Initially, I did not really notice, having never experienced anything like this (I had no knowledge of afterlife matters), and my grieving distracted me from this first encounter: The family was gathered together as we so often did in those first hours, days, and weeks after my husband's death. The grandchildren were simultaneously grieving, playing, and squabbling, when this particular child—aged almost seven at the time—declared "Granddad said, 'I could have the next turn.'"

I recalled thinking, "What a novel way to get your own way!"

Several weeks or possibly months passed. I had been driving with my daughter and this grandchild, catching up on family news. When the car was parked, my daughter suggested that my grandson tell me what he had recently experienced. His first action was to come over from the backseat to kiss my cheek saying, "Granddad said to give Grandma a kiss." He then proceeded to relate to me what he had shared with his mother: that he had seen Granddad, that Granddad had told him that he had a job now (my husband hadn't worked for many years due to a serious health issue), and that his job was protecting Heaven, but he gets a break. He went on to declare that "Granddad now has powers."

This piqued my interest, since I had been receiving many seemingly inexplicable communications from my husband, mostly via third persons. I asked where he had seen his Granddad. He replied matter-of-factly. "In the back of our car."

Many other encounters ensued. He saw Granddad in a cloud, while driving in the car, and he alerted me to Granddad's presence when I was sitting on his family's couch saying, "Granddad is here . . . sitting right behind you."

I asked if he could hug Granddad, and he made the appropriate motions.

Within a short time, the visitations seemed to become more frequent. I can't be sure if the frequency was due to our acceptance of these visits or his willingness to share. However, he now discussed these often, readily, and openly.

On one particular occasion, our family had guests with whom we went to a restaurant for dinner. The grandchildren insisted on having a sleepover, which I was reluctant to host at the time because of a potential shortage of beds. The grandchildren often stayed overnight while Granddad was alive. Since I gave in and allowed them to stay, it necessitated that two of them, including this child, had to sleep in the bed with me. I predicted an uncomfortable night of restless sleep. This grandson, then probably around eight years old, reclined on the bed and abruptly stated, "My heart is beating in the wrong place." With this exclamation, he sat up quickly and looked behind where he had been lying and laughed and said, "I was laying on Granddad."

I asked, "Did you see Granddad earlier in the day when he was visiting our home with his family?"

He replied, "He was out on the side watering the garden," as if it was the most natural thing in the world to him! He added, "He still smokes, you know, but they can't hurt him now."

There were many other occasions he told us of his encounters. One was at another sleepover where I was singing to the children before bedtime, as was the custom. He sleepily mentioned that Granddad had just joined us, "He came through the en suite [adjoining bathroom] and says he loves it when Grandma sings."

However, it was a short time later that he made a request that we don't ever tell anyone he could see spirits. Apparently, his older brother had mentioned it at school, and, consequently, he had been teased.

This grandson requested that he be excluded from religious instruction at school since he had powers and knew all about God already. Curiously, there was a time when he contracted chicken pox and was quite ill, and he lamented that he had lost his powers since he was sick (and could no longer see Granddad). He was chuffed (delighted) at their return after he regained his health.

He said that Granddad, since his passing over, was blue, with legs like a ghost. He wore clothes, could open his eyes, and laugh and smile still. When prompted to pinpoint Granddad's exact location, either in our family home or in his home, he mostly pointed to various areas toward the ceiling. He insisted that Granddad could float. On one particular occasion, when I was visiting his home, I asked if Granddad was there today. Before he answered, he stepped into the hallway and looked around a corner to establish if he could or could not see him. That day, he told me no.

I had been researching the afterlife and had just been acquainted with the term "out-of-body experience." I recall vividly that once when I was caring for these children while their parents were out, it was bedtime and I had been on the computer conducting my research. I went in to kiss the children good-night. This particular child confided in me (spontaneously, with no cues from me), "Do you know Grandma, that when I go to sleep, I can visit Heaven?" He then proceeded to tell me what Heaven was like, for example, houses and animals, all divided into sections that were exclusive to a particular group. He indicated that this group was confined in some way, with fences, to its own area.

In a much later discussion, I asked him to explain to me what Heaven looked like, for example, how the sections were configured. I had been reading somewhere of the seven spheres of the afterlife and wished to determine how his account varied from or confirmed this theory. He attempted to explain, but in order to help, I suggested that he use my set of six acrylic holdalls (containers) to replicate the configuration, as he had experienced it. Rather than place these vertically as I had anticipated, he set them down in a somewhat haphazard fashion, with perhaps two adjacent on the bottom, another one not quite vertically above these, perhaps another two were askew atop this latter one, and so on, with spaces in between. He had previously explained to me that these sections appeared also to be color coded, that is, by the inhabitants.

For example, Granddad was blue and tended to live in the blue zone with other blue and gray spirits. Other areas held inhabitants of red (he explained that this was not such a nice area). Very recently, he informed me that Granddad had an address.

After my husband died, we commemorated special events including his first birthday since his passing, where we shared Granddad's birthday cake. The grandchildren blew out the candles. I asked my grandson if Granddad was present for his party.

He answered "Yes!" and pointed to an area near the ceiling.

I asked if he would mind taking a photo. An orb of light appeared in this photo. I then began to get very excited about orb photography and used my digital camera nightly in my bedroom, capturing many orbs of various sizes and characteristics. One day when my grandson was visiting, I asked him if he would like to see my orb photos. He laughed uproariously and told me that many I had taken were actually dust, but some were spirits and some were spirit creatures. Only a couple were Granddad.

I've asked him whether he's seen any other spirits that were related to us, hoping that he may have seen my dearly loved father. He explained that he didn't know what my father looked like, so he wouldn't know, but he had seen Uncle Nicky with Granddad. Our grandchildren never met Nick, my husband's father in spirit, but they, for some unknown reason, refer to him as Uncle Nicky.

One time he told me matter-of-factly that there were several spirits in my bedroom, at least twelve in my en suite (bathroom) and others in my walk-in robe (closet). There were also several spirit creatures present at various times. This house was purposely built for my family and at the time was less than seven years old. I have heard of ghostly presences in older houses, but I now think that perhaps our world coexists with the spirit world in overlapping dimensions.

This child is one of my seven grandchildren and is the only one who consistently maintains that he sees and converses with Granddad. I've been asked by others, to whom I've related these experiences, if he was particularly close to his Granddad. All the grandchildren were close to Granddad, none more so than the others. The feature that distinguishes this child is his overt sensitivity. He isn't prone to fantasy and is an honest and authentic child who is close to 10 years old.

I am wondrous of the fact that he is generally not perturbed by these encounters with the spirit world, but accepts them readily. I can think of only two occasions where he has displayed fear of such matters: First, around ten years old he was alarmed by a presence: a "white man," that is, completely dressed in white, who was outside his bedroom window for several nights. Second, when he went to the Cirque de Soleil, Varekai, he was greatly distressed and could not remain in the theater.

—*Dell, Australia*

Kirsten's Angel

When my daughter Kirsten was just a baby, I began to notice how she would giggle and coo in her crib after I put her down for the night. The sounds would be coming out of her room for a good thirty minutes, and then she would be asleep. This went on for a few years. The older she got, the more she giggled at night and talked.

When Kirsten reached the age that she could speak in sentences, she informed me that she had a visiting angel friend. This angel would come through the window every night; she even told me the angel's name. I wish I had written it down because it was so beautiful. I have never heard anything even close to that name before. She went on to say, "Mommy, she is so pretty too. She is all white with a white glow and wears a white dress. She is just so pretty."

I didn't know what to make of this information, but she never had any imaginary friends. Where would she get this from if it were made up? Then one night just a few months prior to her going into kindergarten, I heard her call, "Mommy?" from her room. Her voice had an I'm scared or I don't feel well type of tone to it. I ran into her room and she said, "You know that angel friend I have that comes to see me every night?"

I said, "Yeah, what about her?"

"Well she just left, and before she left, she told me that I wouldn't be able to see her anymore, but that she'd still come to visit me every night. I don't understand, what does that mean?"

I sat on the bed next to her, took her hand, and said, "Do you remember my mentioning before that my Mom Mom's mommy was blind and couldn't see?"

Kirsten said, "Yeah."

I said, "Well, just because Mom Mom's mommy couldn't see us, it didn't mean we weren't there. She didn't stop loving us, or talking to us, or believing in us just because she couldn't visibly see us. Plus, you're at the age now where if you tell someone about what you experience or see, such as angels, they may not understand it. So if you need to talk about things like this, you can talk to Daddy and me about them. Remember though, just because you can't see your angel, doesn't mean she isn't there with you."

Kirsten hugged me and was okay with it. She smiled and said that she understood now.

I believe angels watch over babies prior to them being born or at least from birth because when I was in the hospital room trying to deliver Kirsten, the doctor told me to push and the nurses who were coaching me told me to push, but a voice in my head told me repeatedly even louder than the nurses' voices, "*Relax, don't push!*" I listened to the voices and didn't push.

Within seconds I heard the doctor exclaim, "Don't push!"

"I'm not. What's wrong?"

"The baby is facing the wrong way and the cord is around her neck!"

If I had pushed when they all told me to, it could have been fatal.

Then shortly after Kirsten was born, they took her to be weighed in. Everyone left the room, and I felt three presences in the room with me. I didn't visibly see them, but I sensed there were three of them. I believe one was my grandmother. One spoke to me through mind-thought or telepathically saying, "Our job here has been completed and everything will be just fine now. Enjoy your beautiful new baby girl."

I felt such love from this energy. I felt them drift toward the window, and before I felt them go, I smiled and said, "Thank you so much for helping us." I remember tears starting to flow because I was so touched that Heaven sent them to assist in our daughter's birth. I then felt them drift out the window. (I was on the second floor.)

—*Karen Janney, New Jersey*

Link and the Sliding Board

My oldest son, Chris, had to put his fifteen-year-old dog, Link, down. Fifteen years ago, Chris moved to Florida from New Jersey and got Link as a puppy from the SPCA in St. Augustine, Florida.

Link had been with Chris ever since. Link accompanied Chris on I-95 back and forth to New Jersey twice a year, both before Chris got married and after his wife and he had a child, my granddaughter Sophie.

Link was amazing. He really loved my son so much that he would get all excited and stand at the door long before you physically could see Chris's vehicle pulling into the driveway.

Unfortunately, six months ago Link had a stroke and a neurological problem, but Chris was not ready to let him go. He believed that Link was still trying to fight. And as long as Link was trying, he felt he couldn't make the decision to end his life. The vet put him on steroids; the dog had no pain but had extreme difficulty getting up as his hind legs were affected. His sight and hearing were affected too, and he wasn't always in control of his bladder. This went on for several months, but still Chris felt Link wasn't ready. Link would let him know when he was.

Chris had always taken Link to the beach, and Link just loved the water. So Chris decided to take him to the beach one day to see what would happen. Link walked very slowly into the water. The waves were choppy, and as Link was walking back out of the ocean, he fell into the water and couldn't get up. Chris had to pick him up and carry him home. While giving Link a bath that day, Chris came to the sad conclusion that Link was ready.

Chris made an appointment at the vet for that coming Saturday morning, and the family spent Friday evening very tearfully saying their good-byes. The next morning the vet checked him over. He told Chris that the dog was in pain as the steroids were no longer working. Hearing that news made Chris feel better about the decision he had made. He didn't want Link to suffer.

The vet gave Link a sedative while Chris held him on his lap, and in a little while, Link was snoring. Then the vet came back with the final injection, and Link passed very peacefully. While Chris was holding Link, he prayed to his dad in Heaven to get Link when he passed over and to take care of him till he was able to be with him again someday. He also asked Link to give him a sign that he was okay.

That very evening, around dusk, the family was sitting out on their dock when my then nine-year-old granddaughter Sophie suddenly exclaimed, "Daddy, I see Link!"

My son and daughter-in-law turned in the direction Sophie was pointing. Sure enough in the shadows of the early evening, there was the shadowy shape of Link standing with his front paws resting on Sophie's sliding board. They turned on the outdoor light to get a better view, but nothing was there. However, in the dusk, his form was distinctive to all three of them.

Since that miraculous evening, there have been no more signs of Link physically, but we believe he showed his love and thanks to Chris and came to let him know that he was okay now. We are so thankful that little Sophie noticed.

—*Sandi Riley, New Jersey*

CHAPTER 4

Afterlife Encounters
Children Ten to Seventeen Years Old

This chapter shares twenty-four inspirational and uplifting testimonials of children ages ten to seventeen years old who were visited by spirits of their loved ones, angels, pets, and some who had taken their own lives. The children were able to verbalize in more detail to their families what they had witnessed. These afterlife visitations brought immeasurable solace to their bereaved families.

The Appearance of the Giggling Child

We were living in Uruguay when my twin sons, Maxy and Mathias, were born. Eventually, we moved back to the United States. There my little Mathias passed over from a brain tumor on May 5, 2002— the saddest day of my life. Five years later my pain and sadness were still overwhelming. It was Mother's Day and I was feeling terrible. So I knelt in front of my child's picture and asked God to give me a sign that my son was alive and okay with Him. I prayed with all my heart for a gift from Mathias on this special day.

Then a little while after my prayers, I heard a commotion upstairs where my then fourteen-year-old son, Christian, was playing video

his friend Eduardo. They ran out of the room saying to
'Did you see that too? Wow! What *was* that?"

What's the matter? Why are you so excited?"

They said that while they were playing, all of a sudden a child appeared and was running and laughing. The child then hid behind the chair where Christian was and giggled. Then he just disappeared right in front of their eyes. They said he looked exactly like Mathias. Christian said he even giggled the same way he used to. They said he was wearing green overalls, resembling what Mathias often wore when he was younger. The boys were shocked. They both witnessed everything at the same time.

This was truly a gift from Heaven to me, and it has helped tremendously to heal me. I received confirmation that my son was happy and well in answer to my prayers on that Mother's Day. I thank God every day for this ADC and hope that one day I will be able see him this way too.

—*Monica, New Jersey*

Mommy Is Mad at You

My husband Thomas was my son Cory's stepfather. Thomas committed suicide on February 23, 2007, at the age of forty-two. Thomas was an alcoholic who found out a few months earlier that he had cirrhosis and that he was also bipolar. Because he had gone off his medication and was drinking again, it had become very difficult living with him at that point.

My son Cory was eleven years old at that time, and Thomas helped raised him since he was two years old. Thomas always worried that his alcoholism was hurting Cory's childhood years. Thomas loved Cory as if he were his own son. Cory loved his stepfather Thomas with his whole heart and thought of Thomas as if he were his true biological dad.

During the day of Thomas's funeral, Cory put a note in Thomas's coffin that read, "Things We Love: Joe Frazier, wrestling, Xbox, Muhammad Ali, and each other." He signed it, "I love you with all my heart. Love, your son, Cory."

About a week after Thomas passed away, Cory was sitting on my bed watching TV with me. "I have to tell you something," he said.

"What?"

"I saw Thomas the night before."

I looked at him and wondered what he was talking about. "When I had gone to bed, I saw Thomas's face, and it was exactly what Thomas looked like before he had gotten so sick."

He said Thomas told him that he did what he did because he could not stand the pain anymore, and he saw no other choice.

"I love you and Mommy with all my heart," Thomas said.

"You know Mommy is mad at you."

"I know Mommy is mad at me; that's why I came to see you."

"Tom just kept telling me he loved me."

Cory felt so much better after seeing Tom. He told me that Tom was in pain before, and he knew Tom was happy now and I shouldn't be mad at him. It was as if Cory was trying to help me forgive my husband for what he did.

I derived a great deal of comfort from Tom's afterlife visit to my son.

—*Maria Outten Loecker and Cory Outten, Pennsylvania*

I Just Had To

My eleven-year-old son Antal died from an unexpected accident. He immensely loved his big sister Csilla, who was sixteen years old at the time, but as many normal older and younger sibling relationships go, she disdained her little brother and, consequently, felt lots of conflicting emotions of guilt she needed to work through after he died.

The day after he died, Csilla had a very clear vision of Antal, and she chatted with him for about ten minutes. Her conversation with Antal brought her a lot of comfort and closure. She relayed that he appeared right in front of her open eyes in the middle of the afternoon. When she saw him, she said, "Hi!"

"Hi! I'm all right and I love you."

"You know how much I love you, but why did you do the stupid thing that made you die?"

"I don't know. I just had to." (I guess it was simply his time to go back to God.)

Finally, he told her that he would always be around as long as she needed him. She said he sort of lingered in front of her eyes for a while before disappearing completely.

He appeared to her a few times after that, but she said that she no longer felt the need to be in contact with him, so he hasn't appeared to her in a while. These visits not only brought Csilla a great deal of comfort, but they brought comfort to the rest of our family too.

—*Endre Balogh, California*
www.endresphotos.com

Who's the Man in the Doorway?

Our grandson Ryan, at the age of thirteen years old, was at his girlfriend Kim's house one day. While there he saw an older man in the doorway, and Ryan asked Kim who the man was. She told Ryan that she didn't see anyone. Ryan went on to describe the man, and Kim was astounded by what she heard. The man, who Ryan described, was her grandfather. Ryan then asked Kim who the woman was sitting with them on the sofa. Kim was starting to get a little spooked by now because she couldn't see anyone. Ryan described the woman and Kim started to cry. The woman was her grandmother. Her grandparents had passed some time ago, and Ryan hadn't known this, nor had he ever seen a picture of either one of them.

This type of experience is not unusual for Ryan. When Ryan was around twelve years old, he started telling us that he was seeing other spirits, including his Uncle Brian, my son, who was murdered when Ryan was only one and a half years old.

This past summer Ryan and his family came from out of state to Florida to visit me. One day we all went to my son's house in Florida for a family get-together. When Ryan walked into their house, he said that he saw his Uncle Brian, and Uncle Brian was happy that we were all together. Ryan has never been afraid of these sightings. Sometimes he feels his Uncle Brian touching him, and that does not frighten him either. In fact, these contacts make him feel good that his uncle is often with him.

Ryan is very open about what he sees and feels. In fact, Ryan had no idea that some of the other children in the family were also seeing their Uncle Brian. Once Ryan started telling us what he was seeing and hearing, then we told him that similar experiences were happening to his cousins.

I believe that prayer is involved in all of this. I pray all the time for ADCs from our son Brian. I am glad that Brian is sharing his comforting afterlife visits with more of our family members. These experiences are very comforting to my family and me. I thank God all the time for these ADCs.

—*Phyllis Hotchkiss, Florida*

Mike Killed Her

On March 14, 2002, my friend Renee was found dead in her kitchen. It was thought that she had died from choking on food. However, two months later her death was ruled a homicide. We all prayed that justice would be quick and that the right person would be found and dealt with.

Seven months went by, and nothing new had happened in her case. One night my daughter, who was fifteen years old at the time and home for a weekend visit, came running into my room saying, "Ma, Renee said he killed her."

I was shocked and said, "What?"

She explained further. "Renee came to me and she was holding her neck. She said Mike killed her because he was having an affair and wanted her out of the way."

I had kept the details and my personal opinions about Renee's death from my daughter. Also, my daughter was living with her dad in a different state at the time of Renee's death, so she had no prior access to any information in Renee's case. Unbelievably, the very next day after my daughter told me that Mike killed her, I picked up the paper, and sure enough I read that Mike had been arrested for Renee's murder. The paper said that he was having an affair. He was actually heard telling a friend, "She has to go," meaning Renee had to go. He was telling his friends that his girlfriend was his kids' new mommy.

One day my daughter and I went to the cemetery to visit Renee. I could not find where she was buried. While I was driving around the cemetery, my daughter said, "Stop here!"

"No I've checked this plot; she's not here."

"Check again."

So I did and there was Renee's headstone.

My daughter at twenty years old gave birth and named her little girl Lily Renee after my friend Renee. One day she came to me and said, "Mom, let's go to the cemetery to show Lily Renee to Renee, plus I have a feeling something is up with her headstone."

Sure enough, Renee's parents had won the right to change the headstone, as they had wished.

I know my daughter is in contact with the spirit world. She is no longer a kid, but recently my daughter called me at 8:33 P.M. and asked me if I was okay. I didn't understand why she would ask me this. An hour later, I got a call that a close friend of mine had passed at 8:30 P.M.

—Tammy

Smokey and the Bandit

My twin sister Carla and I both owned Pekinese dogs. Carla's dog was named Bandit. My dog is named Scarlette. Carla, who lives with us, suddenly lost Bandit, who was only five years old at the time, to an unexpected illness after being misdiagnosed. This was especially devastating to her because right before Bandit's death, Carla had some other heartbreaking losses. Carla used to say repeatedly to Bandit, "Please don't ever leave me."

After Bandit's sudden passing, Carla started to pray for an afterlife sign from him. I had also asked my deceased grandfather and grandmother to please take care of Bandit now. My son Mikell also prayed to let Bandit know that he loved him.

Eventually my sister adopted a new puppy, which she named Nelson. The day we brought Nelson home from the Humane Society, my dog Scarlette was staring out my sliding glass door and started barking somewhat strangely. I looked through the glass door and saw a dog who looked just like Bandit walking by outside! At first, it caught me off guard, and I thought, whose dog is that? The dog was black and white like Bandit, and though he looked solid, I recognized him to be Bandit's spirit. Later that very day, my then fifteen-year-old son Mikell walked outside and saw Bandit running around, too, for about a full minute.

Then at another time on the date of Scarlette's birthday, Mikell heard Bandit walking around in Carla's bedroom. He heard Bandit's nails clicking loudly on the laminated floor. This was the same sound Bandit always used to make when he was alive and walking on her bedroom floor. When Mikell heard Bandit walking around, he first looked to see if both our dogs Scarlette and Nelson were in the living room with him, and they were. There was no other explanation for this familiar clicking sound, other than Bandit's reappearance, as if to say happy birthday to his sister Scarlette.

My son very openly shared these spiritual experiences with me. I believed him because he wasn't alone in having these spiritual visitations. My twin sister and I had similar experiences with my sister's dog Bandit, and we're so very grateful for them because they've given us a great deal of comfort.

—*Cara Sanders, Georgia*

My Mother's Hand

My daughter Gina is not prone to illness, but whenever she's not feeling well, it's usually because of a bad headache. My mother was a chiropractor and an acupuncturist, and whenever Gina complained of a particularly bad headache, my mother would offer to give her an acupuncture treatment, but Gina would have none of it.

One day a couple of years ago, Gina had a headache that was worse than any of her other headaches. She wasn't getting any relief, so I called my mother and asked her to treat her, though knowing Gina would be resistant. They both have very strong personalities, and sure enough they did battle over the acupuncture treatment. My mother won out; however, she had gotten very upset with Gina's un-cooperative attitude. Gina cried the entire twenty minutes she was going through the treatment. Needless to say, it was Gina's first and last acupuncture treatment, and my mother left feeling very insulted by Gina's adamant stance against acupuncture.

A week after my mother's passing, my then fourteen-year-old daughter Gina had another bad headache. She came to me and asked if she could sleep in my bed with me that night, and I said yes. In the morning her pain wasn't any better and stayed that way for the rest of the day. That evening she asked if she could sleep with me again. This time I asked if she'd be okay in her own bed as I've back issues that are relieved by a lot of repositioning while I sleep. She said she'd be okay in her own bed. The next morning I checked on her, and she said she did feel a little better. But that was all she said about it at the time.

Later that evening, I started to talk about Gina's grandma, and began to cry a little. Gina then said, "Last night I couldn't fall asleep." Then she too quietly started to cry.

I asked her if it was because of her headache, and she shook her head no. I asked if it was because she was thinking about Grandma, and she said no. In a voice just barely above a whisper, with tears slowly rolling down her cheeks, she told me last night she was praying that Grandma and Lady, who was our dog we had put down a few days after my mom passed, were okay. She asked God please to take care of them and to make sure they were okay. (It is notable that my children have never had any formal religious training, just a strong spiritual sense based on my upbringing, so I was somewhat surprised and proud that she turned to God with her prayer.)

She continued to tell me that while lying there, with her eyes closed, trying to fall asleep, she felt a hand patting her shoulder. I was trying to determine if this *hand* may have been something other than my mother's hand.

I asked, "Were the blankets twisted and rubbing against you?" She said, "No."

"Was it just a couple of pats?" I was still thinking maybe it just felt like a hand.

"No, it wouldn't stop!"

She said the hand just kept patting her and patting her. I asked her how long this went on, and she said until she fell asleep. I then asked her if she opened her eyes, and she said she didn't because she was afraid to. I asked her if she felt that it was Grandma, letting her know she was okay, and comforting Gina because of her headache, and she said yes, she did think it was her grandma.

Although I selfishly wish that I could've had this type of communication from my mom, just knowing that my mom loved and cared for Gina so much that she visited her, especially while she wasn't feeling well, was testament of her love beyond measure for both of us. I felt comforted, knowing my mom was still watching over, not just me, but also my children. Since my mother's last attempt to treat Gina with acupuncture when she had such a bad headache was not so gentle, rather a war of wills, it was particularly meaningful to me that my mother would come to "treat" her in a much gentler manner.

Back then I never read anything about ADCs and never even considered the possibility of afterlife contacts. Not long after my mother's afterlife visit, I found myself wondering if there might be any books on this subject that could explain what Gina had experienced. As I soon discovered, there is a plethora of information on this topic. In many of the books, I was surprised to find that often the ADCs came because of prayer. It is because of our love that is sent to our loved ones via prayer that initiates the contact in many of these instances or, at least, allows us to be open to receiving the communication.

—*Paula Leach*

The Pregraduation Hug

My son Jonathan was seventeen years old when he died on December 11, 2005. He had spent the night at a friend's house, and the next morning we found out, to our shock and horror, that the house had burned down. My son and his two best friends perished in the fire. The homeowner, his son, and another boy escaped.

My son's graduation ceremony from high school was scheduled to be five months later in May 2006. For the ceremony, the school principal was going to be giving out diplomas to a member of each family of the three boys who died. We had to decide who from our family was going to walk onto the stage and accept our son's diploma. We needed to let the school know ahead of time so that they could announce the name of the family member accepting his diploma. Much to my relief, my then eleven-year-old daughter Kaitlyn immediately volunteered.

The night before the graduation ceremony, Kaitlyn told me about an amazing experience that happened to her. She was sitting on her bed watching TV when her door slowly creaked open all by itself and a very cold breeze came traveling through the room. Right after that, she felt someone pushing gently down on her shoulders as if she were being hugged. I asked her if this scared her and she said no. Yet at any other time, the mere opening of her door would send her into a scared frenzy.

As she was telling me about this strange but peaceful experience, I immediately knew it was my son visiting giving her a big hug around her neck from behind, as he always did. I felt he was thanking her for being brave enough to accept his diploma for him.

After I had told her my thoughts, she was never sad another day about her brother's death. She suddenly had the realization and confirmation that her brother would always be there, and she was thrilled that he was proud of her.

—*Carole Barrett*
www.jonathan-barnes.memory-of.com

Ohmmm

I have had a number of spiritual contacts from my dad who passed over two years ago, when I was twelve years old.

One day I was feeling very sad because I was missing my dad so much. I decided that I wasn't going to go to school that day. As I sat on my bed crying, I suddenly saw my dad shedding a tear. His tear was a silver color. I then thought to myself, "Why should I be crying?" So I stopped my crying and got ready to go to school. Seeing my dad just then really helped me feel so much better.

Recently my friend, her mom, my mother, and I all went to a crystal bowl meditation. There you listen to the sounds of the crystal bowl. It is wonderfully relaxing. The instructor mentioned that we might see or experience *things* during the meditation. I had a great time and even had a one-on-one talk with my dad during it. When I first saw my dad during the meditation, he grabbed my hand and I heard him say, "I love you."

I think he did this so I wouldn't feel frightened by his appearing to me. He was sitting in a red chair like a king would sit on, and we were on clouds together. During this time the instructor was saying "Ohmmm," and my dad was being silly. He was imitating the instructor and joking around with me.

I also saw my dad one day while eating breakfast. My dog saw him first. She was sound asleep and drooling all over me, then she suddenly perked up and looked over at the hallway. I looked too and I saw my dad. I saw him walk into the kitchen. He looked taller than usual this time, and he had a very bright white glow all around him.

I know my daddy is here and that he loves me with all his heart. My daddy is around my mother and me all the time and sends signs almost every day.

—*Jenna-Lee Sheehan, Florida*

William Nelson

My grandfather William Nelson was the greatest. He was a decorated World War II veteran who flew on a B-17 as a tail gunner. My grandfather flew sixty-three missions and was also a crew chief on the *Mighty Fortress* in the North African campaign. Grandfather would tell me about all kinds of adventures he had during the war, like the time he got to dance with Betty Grable on the *Queen Mary* going back home from England. He later flew as crew chief on General Eisenhower's B-17 during noncombat transport missions, and once my grandfather was on a newsreel with Eisenhower. My grandfather very sadly lost his crew at the Death March at Bataan, when he stayed behind in Savannah to see his first child being delivered, who was my aunt.

I lost my grandfather on May 20, 2005. He was almost eighty-eight years old. He was very, very fond of my son Mikell. And my son loved him too. My son was fifteen years old at the time, and this was the first death he had ever experienced, so it really bothered him.

Less than a month after my grandfather's passing, he came to my son. The date he appeared to my son happened to be on June 10, 2005, which was my grandfather's eighty-eighth birthday. My son was playing video games with a friend. When the friend got up to go out of the room, my son saw someone out of the corner of his eye in the room with him. He looked closer in that direction and recognized my grandfather standing there. Grandfather looked solid and young, about the age of forty. Mikell was utterly amazed! This was very healing for all of us.

—Cara Sanders, Georgia

The White Figure

My husband's brother Tom died of cancer in 1995. It wasn't a sudden death, though we knew he didn't have long to live. My daughter April was thirteen years old at the time. When April came home from school the day of his passing, I sat her down and told her about her uncle's death. She was very upset, as we all were, so my husband and I decided it wouldn't be a good idea for her to go to his funeral.

A few days after Tom's funeral, April told us that she had dreamed of her Uncle Tom, but in the dream she couldn't see his face, just the back of him. About a week after that, April told us she was in her bedroom with the door closed. She heard who she thought was us calling her name from downstairs. When she opened her bedroom door to respond to our calling her, she said she saw a white figure go from the hall into our bedroom and slowly disappear.

April said she felt for sure it was her Uncle Tom letting her know he was all right and in Heaven. We told her that we never did call her name that night from downstairs, and we believe, as she did, that the white figure was her Uncle Tom and that he was giving her a sign he was okay.

—Beverly Heaney, New Jersey

Cool It

My then fourteen-year-old granddaughter Samantha was always afraid of her younger brother's ability to see the spirits of the deceased. She never experienced anything herself until right after her Grampy Duane died. One night she was lying on her bed watching TV when all of a sudden her fan blades spun around twice and then abruptly stopped. She screamed, and her mother Sheryl went into her room thinking it was a bug that made her scream. Sheryl asked Samantha what was wrong, and Samantha told her what happened with the fan. Now she was really scared! Sheryl told Samantha that she could sleep between her dad Mike and her for the night. They have a huge king-size bed.

When Samantha crawled into bed with her mother, her dad Mike was still in the shower. Samantha happened to glance over to the side of the bed where her dad usually sleeps. She was startled to see a man's body peacefully lying there, but it wasn't her dad's! Then the body disappeared.

When my son Mike got out of the shower, Sheryl and Samantha described what had just happened. Mike, who is a believer in ADCs, told Samantha that he believed Grampy made the fan spin around in her room on its own. He reminded Samantha that she had been reprimanded earlier because she and her boyfriend had been kissing. He said that her Grandpa Duane also wanted them to cool it with their recent hugging and kissing. Mike said the man's body was her Grampy's letting her know that he was watching over her from Heaven. During that evening Mike woke up feeling a peaceful yet unseen hand on his chest. He knew that it was his father's.

It is comforting for everyone in our family when any one of us has an ADC. We always share them with each other, and we are never afraid to talk about them. Prayer plays a big part in our lives enabling us to get through anything.

—*Phyllis Hotchkiss, Florida*

Work Shirt and Levi's

Ever since my beloved dad passed over at the age of sixty-six, we had been praying for afterlife signs (ADCs) from him. About three months after my dad's passing, my family and I moved in with my mother while we were in the process of looking for a house to buy. One day my then twelve-year-old son Jon had been outside playing in front of my parents' house when he came running into the house all out of breath. Very excitedly he started telling us that there was a man outside on the deck. We weren't expecting anyone, so we walked outside to greet the visitor. However, no one was on the deck when we got there. Since my parents' house is on nine acres in a rural area, we asked Jon more questions about the man who vanished into thin air.

Jon described the man as a short man with brown hair, wearing a blue work shirt and Levi's. Jon told us that he said hi to the man, thinking he was there to see my mother. The man smiled at Jon and just stood there not saying anything. That's when Jon came running into the house to get us.

Knowing that my dad usually wore a blue work shirt and Levi's, my mom went into her room and came out with a picture of my dad of when he was a young man.

Jon said, "That's the man!"

"That's a picture of your grandpa when he was much younger."

"Wow, that's creepy."

Jon had only known his grandpa as a much older looking man. We lived in Washington State when Jon was born, and my dad lived in Southern California. My kids usually only got to see my dad about once a year. Sadly, my dad was diagnosed with nasal cancer, which eventually spread to his brain and was the cause of his passing. The cancer treatments took a great toll on him, and most of his treatments involved his face. The last time Jon saw his grandpa, he didn't even look like himself, which explains why Jon didn't recog-

nize him when he appeared to him as a transformed young and
healthy spirit.

Over the next five years, Jon saw his grandpa a number of times
outside around my mother's house and outside our house too. When
Jon would see him, he would always say, "Hi grandpa," without
missing a beat and continued on with whatever he was in the middle
of doing. Jon felt very comforted knowing his grandpa was watching
over him and so did I.

—Brenda Anderson, Idaho

Patent Leather Shoes

My beloved father Stanley was called home to the Lord in February
2000. He would often give me afterlife signs to let me know that he
could still see and hear us and was still a part of our lives.

One evening around midnight, a few months after my dad's passing, my then fourteen-year-old daughter Jamie came running downstairs from her bedroom. She ran into the room I was in and
breathlessly asked me if I'd heard that loud banging of a door. I hadn't.
She told me about a dramatic event that had just occurred upstairs
in her bedroom. She explained that while she was lying in her bed,
with her door closed, she had suddenly seen a pair of men's patent
leather shoes appear under her closed bedroom door. Yet, the bottom of Jamie's door practically touches the floor, which would leave
no room for a physical pair of men's shoes to fit underneath!

She further explained that as quickly as the shoes appeared to her,
they disappeared. Then in the next instant, she heard a loud noise
down the hall, sounding like someone had just very loudly slammed
the door shut to her brother's bedroom. Jamie said it sounded like
the person had gone in to look at her brother and slammed the door
behind him. Yet there was no possible natural explanation for how
the man could in one instant be at Jamie's bedroom door and then
the next instant be transported so quickly into her brother's room

down the hall. The rooms are just too far apart. Plus, the slamming of the door didn't wake her brother.

I had the most delightful feeling that the man, who was supernaturally able to fit those patent leather shoes under a door, was my dad. However, just to reassure my daughter, I went upstairs with her to search for the man who she thought was somewhere upstairs. After a careful search, no one turned up. My son was still fast asleep. Jamie said that the sound she heard was so loud that it would've awoken her brother. So it must've been a sound only meant for Jamie's ears to hear that night. I certainly didn't hear it, and she said it was so loud that I should've been able to.

Jamie and I talked about the event, and we both concluded that this visitor was her grandfather, my dad. This was so very comforting to me at the time to know that my dad watches over my children. I had to smile thinking about how theatrical Daddy was in making his presence known to Jamie so that he could really get her undivided attention. And it worked! It is great knowing that my dad still has his sense of humor too. I still smile about it today. I thank God for allowing these wonderful visits from my dear dad.

—*Christine Duminiak*

Angel Ann

My stepniece Ann had Down syndrome and her intellectual age was believed to be comparable to a twelve-year-old. I was blessed to be her caretaker on many occasions. Ann was very particular about the person who took care of her though, and I am so glad that she and Father God entrusted me to care for her those few times when her mother, Lynn, had to be away. Ann taught me more than anyone else about the power of God's love. Ann always had a smile on her face and always seemed to care more about others than herself. I felt I was in the presence of an angel.

Ann seemed to talk to angels all the time. One of her angels was a fellow named Ernie, which was her mother's brother who had passed. Ann had never met him and did not know he was her mother's brother. She talked with Ernie often. When her mother's dad was nearing the end of his time here, Ernie told Ann that Papa Joe would be okay. We found that to be so comforting.

It was very hard for Ann to go anywhere, due to her health problems. These trips always included taking her wheelchair, oxygen, and other health-related items. One day Lynn, Ann's mom, was going out for a trip with Ann; she got her loaded into the car, and as they were leaving, Lynn realized that Ann was not breathing and had lapsed into unconsciousness. She panicked and immediately drove her to the hospital. On the way over, she was calling Ann's name over and over, hoping that it would bring her back to consciousness. As they were nearing the hospital, Ann suddenly woke up and said, "I'm fine, Mom."

The next day the family was talking about what had happened. Lynn asked, "Ann, could you tell me what actually did happen?"

Ann said, "Mom, I went to sleep and then I told God I wasn't ready to die. Then an angel kissed me on the head, gave me a cold drink of water, and said, 'It's not your time yet.'"

Eventually God did call Ann to Heaven to stay for good. We all started receiving signs from this little angel soon thereafter.

One day Lynn and I were at a rodeo. We were thinking about Ann and remembering how much she loved all animals, but especially horses. I did not know that Lynn was cloud watching at the same time I was. When I looked up to the sky, there was Ann's face with angel wings behind her. This cloud formation stayed for a good fifteen minutes. Suddenly Lynn and I looked at one another; she had tears streaming down her face and said, "Do you see what I see?"

I said, "Yes, I do."

We both cried tears of joy because Ann was saying once again, "I'm fine, Mom."

—Kay

Anna! Anna! Anna!

On September 20, 2003, my lovely twenty-year-old daughter Liz passed away. We were heartbroken. She was a sophomore at the University of Minnesota. Just nineteen days earlier, we had moved into an off-campus duplex she was sharing with six of her friends.

Liz's twentieth birthday was coming up on September 12. As part of her birthday present, I gave her four tickets to the Minnesota Wild hockey game for the night of September 19. I had won the tickets at work and knew we couldn't use them.

Liz and three roommates went to the game that night. Afterward they went over to the parents' place of one of their roommates and partied until approximately 2 A.M. The four of them returned to the duplex, and they decided to stay out on their porch and continue partying until almost 4:00 A.M. At 4:50 A.M. the fire call came in. One of the roommates, Fik, survived the fire by diving headfirst out of a two story window. Tragically, Liz, Amanda, and Brian all died of smoke inhalation.

The following year, the month of September arrived—the dreaded month. I had been thinking about it since June. Wondering, how would I get through this horrible month? First, we had to go through her birthday on the twelfth. She would have been twenty-one. Well, that would have been some party, I thought to myself. She would have been legal. It was a day I had waited a long time for. Now, it meant nothing. Eight days later, we would mark the first anniversary of her death. But I was positive she would give me a sign at some point during that month. After all, it was a big, important month. Surely she would come through for me.

Then on September 20, my younger daughter, Anna, who was seventeen, was awakened from a very deep sleep when she heard her sister, Liz, hollering, "Anna!" over and over again. It was loud enough to wake her. She knew without a doubt it was Liz's voice that had been yelling out, "Anna!" "Anna!" "Anna!" I finally got my sign through my daughter Anna. This incident coincided with the one-year anniversary of Liz's death. Liz knew this was going to be an especially difficult day for all of us, and she wanted us to know that she was aware of this, and she was with us trying to comfort us. And she did. My girl was still alive and well and keeping in touch.

—*Kim Wencl, Minnesota*
kimwencl.com

Nalah, Our German Shepherd

For eight wonderful years, we had a sweet German shepherd we loved named Nalah. My daughter was especially close to her. Nalah slept in my husband's and my bedroom every night.

My daughter was ten years old at the time that Nalah crossed over in August 2008. Nalah passed from cancer. I was there when they put her to sleep. I could not bear the thought of her dying all by herself. So I sat there and held her as they injected her with the medication to put her to sleep. I have never cried so much and so hard. After she passed, I continued to sit there and hold her sweet face in my arms. We do miss her still.

My daughter was so upset and continually cried after Nalah's passing. She missed her greatly. It was heartbreaking to see her so sad. A few nights after Nalah had crossed over, my daughter excitedly said that she smelled Nalah in our bedroom. I had not noticed the scent before she said something to me, but then I too smelled Nalah. Smelling the strong scent of Nalah in our bedroom has happened on many occasions for almost a year now.

Also, Nalah loved to be outside during the day. Since Nalah has crossed over, my daughter has also heard Nalah's distinctive barking outside.

These visits from time to time have been very comforting for our family and have helped us just knowing that Nalah is okay and she loves us.

—*Lynette, Georgia*

The Premonition

Jim and Judy Collier's twenty-six-year-old son Kyle died as the result of an automobile accident in Baton Rouge, Louisiana, on April 25, 1996.

On the day of Kyle's accident, the Colliers' fourteen-year-old granddaughter, Jaclyn, was to arrive from Washington State for a two-week visit.

After Jim and Judy picked her up at the airport, the Colliers and Jaclyn were in a joyful mood, discussing all that they had planned to do for the next two weeks. While driving down Kenilworth Parkway, only a few blocks from the Colliers' home, Judy Collier spotted Kyle's white Bronco traveling in the opposite direction. She knew that Kyle had made plans to go out that evening, so she wasn't surprised to see him.

Judy pointed out Kyle's car to Jaclyn, and Jaclyn spontaneously blurted out, "He will probably be in an accident."

Jim and Judy looked at each other. Judy wondered, "Why would she say that?"

It bothered Jaclyn that she'd said it and hoped that it wasn't a premonition of things to come. Jaclyn told her grandparents she didn't know why she'd said that her Uncle Kyle will probably be in an accident, and it bothers her to this day. Sadly, Jaclyn's premonition did come true.

Jaclyn had never attended a funeral before, and needless to say she was very emotional at her Uncle Kyle's funeral. It was difficult for her to look at her Uncle Kyle in the casket.

The Colliers' daughter, Jill, arrived for the funeral, and Jaclyn went back to Washington with her mother the day after the funeral. Within one week of Kyle's funeral, Jaclyn telephoned her grandmother. She wanted to share the dream she had of Kyle. She said it was a "very real" dream, and she knew Kyle was really there. Apparently in her dream, Kyle was lying in the casket, and while she was looking at him, he suddenly sat up. He kept telling her, "I'm okay.

I'm okay." This dream brought Jaclyn a lot of comfort, and she re-members it very vividly even today.

A few months later, Jaclyn called her grandparents again. Jim and Judy weren't home, so Jaclyn left a message on their answering ma-chine. She sounded very excited when she said, "I was sitting on the sofa, about fifteen feet from the fireplace. We have seven picture frames with family pictures that are sitting on the mantel. At the same time, for no apparent reason, all the picture frames fell to the floor—all the picture frames except for the frame that held Uncle Kyle's photograph."

Jaclyn thought this event was weird, and she immediately thought that her Uncle Kyle did this. Mysteriously, none of the frames broke, and Jaclyn felt close to Kyle when this happened. She even felt his presence.

Judy and Jim are happy that Kyle was able to bring comfort to his niece Jaclyn, and because of these experiences, Jaclyn has become more aware of the wonders of the spiritual world.

—*Judy Collier*
Author, Quit Kissing My Ashes

Is This My Sister?

My mother told me a story about what happened to me when I was younger. When I was three years old, I told my mother's friend, who was babysitting, that I'm having a baby sister. My mother's friend was overly excited and congratulated my mother on being pregnant. My mom was puzzled; she wasn't pregnant. A few weeks later she found out that she was pregnant with a baby girl after all. Sadly, the baby died at birth, but I always believe that she's with us.

My father passed from cancer in 2005, when I was almost thir-teen years old. At the time, I started seeing a little girl around the house who looked to be about ten years old. That is how old my sister would have been if she had lived. There was one night when a little girl woke me, poking my nose and saying "Wake up!"

I swatted her away and said, "Leave me alone!" But she continued to try to get me up. When I opened my eyes, I saw a laughing little girl who resembled my father's and mother's traits, and then she soon disappeared. I've seen her couple of times after that.

One time I walked outside when it was dark, and and a strange thing occurred. The sky suddenly turned a different color—into a sunset—and trees were mysteriously popping up everywhere.

It took me a few seconds to realize that my surroundings were changing into a forest right before my eyes. This was really curious because we live in Florida, and we have mostly palm trees. Soon I was standing on a path that led to a clearing; there were trees surrounding an empty lot. It looked like a large area of land that a house could be built on. At the end of the trail was the same little girl smiling at me in a pretty white dress, who I felt was my sister who had died. It was a very peaceful feeling seeing her there. Then I heard my mother calling my name, and I snapped out of the trance. I told my mother all about it. She then told me about how she was thinking of buying land in the forest beside my aunt's house in Massachusetts. That summer when I visited my aunt, I saw the area where we would be building a house. It was the same forest in which I saw the little girl when I was in my trance.

Because of my own experiences, I'm a strong believer in ADCs even if it's just a simple hello or a warning. If spirits want to get a message across, for some reason, they will.

—*Jenna-Lee Sheehan, Florida*

A Message of Love

Let me start by introducing myself. My name is Jonna Casoli, it's 2009, I'm fourteen years old, and I live in southern Maine with my mom, dad, and brother. Now I'm not the main focus of this story, my grandmother, Rose Marie Casoli, is.

Before I was born, she was diagnosed with the horrible, incurable disease known as Alzheimer's. Ever since I was a baby, she's been the best grandmother she could be to me, constantly loving and caring, but this thing in her brain was slowly taking her away from my whole family and me. I have a few wonderful memories of the times we had together before her Alzheimer's made her forget everything, but one time in particular stands out more than the rest.

I remember going on vacation to the beach with my grandma, grandpa, Auntie Christine, dad, mom, and brother, Mike. I don't remember much about the whole vacation, but I do remember all of us standing on the balconies of our hotel rooms, holding sparklers and watching the waves crash on the shore. My grandma would put her arms around my brother and me and sing. I don't know whether it was her favorite song, but she loved to sing "Miss America," and she'd sing it proudly for everyone on the face of this earth to hear. This is one of the happiest memories I have of my grandmother, and I wouldn't trade it for the world.

Not all the memories were good, especially near the end of her time with us. In January 2009 she was hospitalized for pneumonia. When I went to see her in the hospital, I had to fight back my tears. Grandma was asleep, and other than the shallow movements of her chest rising and falling with each breath, you couldn't tell if she was alive or dead. Although it hurt to see her like that, I'd become detached because in most of my memories she couldn't talk, walk, or eat without being fed. This made it hard to remember the good times.

The doctors tried their hardest to stop the pneumonia, but they couldn't, and she was sent home to live with Grandpa. She had to stay in a hospital bed in my aunt's old room so that it would be easier to care for her. I only saw her a few more times after she returned home. Usually on Sundays my family made the one-and-a-half hour ride down to Massachusetts to visit. One of those days will be burned into my memory forever.

Every time I entered her room, I felt like crying, but I always went in to say good-bye to my grandma. My aunt was feeding her ice cream and singing along to a song on the radio, being her typical crazy self. That night, Grandma looked particularly bad. Her eyes were closed, and it seemed like she was in a coma, even though she could swallow her frozen treat.

We returned from our long ride home at 9:00 P.M. Since I had school the next day, I washed up and got ready for bed. That night I had one of the best dreams I'd had in years. I saw my grandma sitting on my aunt's old bed across the room from the hospital bed she'd been staying in. She looked beautiful. Her hair was black, her natural color, and up in the bun she always wore. She was even dressed like she used to, in her sparkly black shirt with a little pin on the right. These were the two items I remember her wearing the most. The best accessory she had was shining through the brightest—her beautiful smile! I hadn't seen that smile in years due to her disease, but there it was as clear as if I weren't dreaming. The dream ended as abruptly as it began, and a different one started, it was another dream about my grandmother.

This time I was looking out of my bedroom window when my grandmother walked into the scene holding my two dogs, Ben and Dezyl, on leashes. When I smiled at her, she smiled back and said, "Jonna, I want you to know that I love you so much, and I want you to take care. Please send this message to the rest of the family. I love you."

I woke up to the sound of my alarm, went to the kitchen, and told my dad about the dreams. He smiled the sort of smile that said I'm pretending to be happy, said good-bye, and left for work. Later when I told my mom about my dreams, she said, "Oh really? That's strange."

Throughout the day I kept thinking about how strange the

dreams were, but I never thought about what they could really mean. When my brother and I returned from school that day, my mom sat down with us in the living room and said, "Jonna, you had those dreams for a reason, Grandma passed away last night."

So many things went through my mind, but what stood out most was that she chose me to send her final message to. She gave me her message from the next life, probably only moments after she'd passed. My dreams weren't just dreams.

Hearing her say that she loved me and knowing that she was not really gone were the two things that kept me going through the wake and funeral. After the many torturous years of trying to battle the disease that stole her memory, she was finally able to escape her prison. Now whenever I miss her, I just remember her smile in that first dream. A smile that said, "I'm free."

—*Jonna Casoli, Maine*

Jon Saved My Life

I was a single mom who was raising my son Jonathan (Jon). I was struggling and, perhaps, made a naïve choice when I married a man who did not turn out to have as good a character as I had thought. Together though, we had a wonderful daughter who we named Kaitlyn. But Kaitlyn's biological father turned into a terrible, evil man who was abusive and mean. My son Jon never liked him. After I finally left Kaitlyn's father, Jon told me horrible stories about things he did to him when I was at work. Jon vowed that he would always keep his sister safe from that man, no matter what.

As time went on, I met and married a wonderful and caring man who has been a terrific stepfather to both my children. Disaster struck our family when my seventeen-year-old son Jon died in a house fire while staying overnight at a friend's house. My husband and I lost our beautiful son, and Kaitlyn lost her protector. We were devastated.

It was only two weeks after Jon passed away when something incredible happened. One morning, Kaitlyn was having a very vivid dream about her brother. In the dream Jon was trying very hard to get her attention, and he told her, "Hurry, we have to wake up mom and tell her; we have to get her attention!"

Well, as a result of her deep sleep and this intense and absorbing dream, Kaitlyn did not hear her alarm clock go off, and she missed her bus for school. So my husband, Kaitlyn's stepfather, told her not to worry and to go ahead and get dressed; just meet him at the car, and he would drive her to school. When they arrived at the school, they discovered that all the doors were locked, and she could not get in. This was highly unusual. So my husband used his cell phone to call the school office to find out why.

The secretary in the office told him to put Kaitlyn in the car and take her home right way because the police were on their way; the school was put on "lock-down." When he pressed her for more information, she told him that Kaitlyn's biological father had shown up at the school. He was intoxicated, and appeared to be on drugs, and was walking around the school pushing people down and yelling that he wanted his daughter immediately.

Finally, Kaitlyn's biological dad left the building before the police got there. Because of his actions though, and to Kaitlyn's enormous relief, he was put in jail. He is not allowed to see her. Worrying about seeing her father has been hanging over her head for a long time. She never wanted to be in his company.

To this day, we all believe—we *know*—that Jon was the one who saved his sister's life that day. Had she been on the school bus, he most likely would have grabbed Kaitlyn and kidnapped her before she went into the building. In fact, the janitor reported seeing a suspicious-looking car with tinted windows in the school parking lot around 6 A.M. that day. So we believe he was laying in wait for her to come off the bus.

Kaitlyn has since become more relaxed, and she is excelling in school better than ever now. Her brother kept his promise, even from Heaven, that he would always keep her safe from *that* man. This is an affirmation for all of us that Jon will always be with us.

—*Carole Barrett*

www.jonathan-barnes.memory-of.com

We Got to Kiss Adam Again

My wife Marilena; our three children, Livia, Nicolas, and Adam; and I all took a family vacation to the Dominican Republic in January 2005. While there on January 5, 2005, we went on an excursion to the Damajagua waterfalls. It was advertised to be safe for children.

At the point of the excursion when it was our eleven-year-old son Adam's turn to go downstream with the current, he had a smile on his face. To our horror, he was pulled by the current into this hollow area and sucked under. Adam was a strong swimmer, but it did not matter on that day. All attempts to resuscitate him failed. Livia begged them to "keep trying, keep trying." Nicolas looked on in shock. My poor children saw their brother die in front of them. Words just cannot describe our feelings. Since that day, we have done all that we can to warn others of the dangers of the falls and to help other children through Adam's memorial fund, and to try to heal ourselves.

Anytime we get an afterlife contact from Adam, we rejoice. It helps tremendously with our loss and sorrow. And we have had many over the years.

There was one back on January 9, 2007, after many nights of praying to God to give me a dream visit from Adam that I finally received one, as did our then eleven-year-old daughter Livia that same night. In fact a third person got a sign from Adam that same day.

In my dream, Adam was back again with us, but we all knew that he had died. In spite of this, we were wondering whether to send Adam to school even though it would freak his classmates out because they knew he had died. Adam said that he would be too far behind in his schooling. In this same dream, I was on my way to work and thought of taking Adam to work with me. I was afraid that if I went to work without him, and came back that night, he would be gone again as in so many previous dreams. Deep down inside I knew this visit would not last. The most joyful part of the dream is that I was able to hold, hug, and kiss Adam on the side of his warm head. It felt so real and so good.

When I woke up, I was in such a great mood. I shared the dream with my family. My daughter Livia told me, to my delight and astonishment, that she also had a dream that very night, and she got to hug and kiss her bother Adam too! We were amazed! This was further validation that the dream was a real visit from Adam. Livia could not remember all the details of the dream but the main and vivid point that stayed with her was that she got to kiss and hug her brother again.

At school that day, where my wife Marilena works, she was feeling down and talking to a teacher who was comforting her about Adam. Marilena watched this teacher flip through some folders, and this teacher suddenly came across a folder called Adam's Story. Marilena and the teacher looked at each other in amazement, and both agreed it was a sign from Adam.

—*Andrew Vitaterna, Ontario*
www.adamvitaterna.com

A Peek into Heaven

My grandmother and I were very close. I was her first grandchild. One evening my parents were unexpectedly called away from our home in Rochester, New York. I was already tucked into bed and was being watched by a babysitter. I was five years old at the time.

As I drifted off to sleep, I felt my bedroom transform itself into an entirely different setting. Not knowing whether I was dreaming or lying in some dreamlike state, I immediately sat up in my bunk bed and saw my grandmother standing before me with two very hand-some gentlemen, one at each side. She was wearing what appeared to be a goldish white ball gown, and she was standing at the base of a spiral staircase in a Victorian-style mansion. The scene resembled something out of a period movie. In the background were other peo-ple who were elegantly dressed and mingling with one another in a partylike atmosphere. I remember that my grandmother looked years younger and remarkably beautiful, with a big smile on her face. Gone were the glasses, wrinkles, and failing body.

She told me that she had come to me to show me what Heaven looked like so that, someday, when it was my turn to join her, I would not be afraid. Then, in what seemed to be too short a time to stay with her, she turned and started up the staircase with her male escorts.

When my parents returned home that evening, my mother tip-toed into my bedroom, sat at the side of my bunk bed, and told me that she had something sad to tell me. She was absolutely amazed when I turned to her and said, "It's okay, Mom, Grandma was here earlier to say good-bye and showed me Heaven. She is very happy and wants you to know that she is living in a wonderful place." Needless to say, my mom almost fell off the bed!

But the story does not end here. Exactly twelve years later, as a teenager, I fell strangely ill. Most medical professionals just brushed it off as a bad case of puberty. But one night, I had another waking dream. This time I was standing in front of our bathroom mirror. Suddenly, my grandma appeared in the mirror and told me that I was *very* sick. She said that I must convince my doctors to take an-other look at me or that I would die very soon. I was so startled, but thanks to my open-minded mom (a registered nurse) and an under-standing family doctor who took another look at me, I was diag-nosed with a rare and deadly cancer.

Much later, and after a successful course of treatment, my doctor confided in me that had I *not* come to see him when I did, I would have been terminal in six weeks!

—*Patricia Whelan, Connecticut*

I Didn't Go Anywhere, Baby Girl

I lost my husband three years ago in a motorcycle accident. We had been married almost two and a half years. My husband and I had a baby together, and I also have two children from a previous relationship. We were a very close and loving family.

A little over a year after my husband's accident, my daughter Samantha, who was almost eleven at the time, came running in my room to tell me that she had just seen Dad!

Our bedroom doors were right across the hall from each other. My daughter explained that she had walked down the hallway, and just as she passed my doorway, she saw my husband sitting on his side of the bed looking out the window. She said she didn't see all of his body, just his left side. She explained in great detail how he was just sitting there very solemnly looking out of the window with his hands folded in his lap. He was wearing the normal type of clothes he always used to wear—jeans and a T-shirt.

Knowing that our loved ones communicated with us by also sharing their emotions, I asked her what feelings she got from the experience. She said that she felt as if Dad knew he was gone, and it made him sad. That sitting on his side of the bed gave him comfort.

Samantha had also had a dream in which she saw my husband and asked him where he had gone. He simply looked down at her and smiled and said, "I didn't go anywhere, baby girl. I've always been right by your side."

I thank my husband for appearing to her. It may have scared her a little bit, but at least she was lucky enough to have a clear reminder that Dad was still very much here and still a part of our lives.

—Jennifer and Samantha Scott, Arkansas

PART III

Religious Concerns and Spiritual Gifts

CHAPTER 5

Does the Bible Permit Spirit Communication?

❦ Many from diverse belief systems and countries around the world welcome afterlife contacts from the spirits of their loved ones. They derive a great deal of comfort, joy, and healing from receiving a visit or sign.

Since 1998 when I first entered the field of spiritual bereavement support, I have been contacted by people of many different faiths who have been gifted to be able to see, hear, and communicate with spirits. The only spiritually gifted people from whom I hear a great deal of angst and conflict are those who belong to the Christian faith. (This includes Catholics.) Because an overwhelming majority of Americans identify with a Christian religion, 82 percent according to a 2007 Gallup poll, and because this is the only religious group of people who consistently sought more reassuring answers, I felt I needed to address their specific concerns, fears, and experiences.

Some Christians, who have shared their mystical encounters with me, have also expressed sadness and isolation because they had experienced condemnation by their church leaders and members. Some of their well-meaning churches did not recognize their spiritual gifts as being from God. Some were told that all these contacts were from Satan and were warned to cease and desist. As a consequence of the criticism received, some of these God-loving and very gifted Christians are turned off by their churches, and some have even left their Christian faith. Yet these people wholeheartedly believed that their gifts were from God's Holy Spirit, and these gifts should be pursued even if their church leaders did not agree with them.

It is distressing to me that even in the twenty-first century that people are still being judged negatively for what they believe God has gifted them to do on earth. Although today they are not being physically persecuted and burned at the stake like Saint Joan of Arc was in the 1400s, there is still a great deal of fear, discrimination, and misunderstanding concerning this particular spiritual gift.

Some of the reasons for this modern-day condemnation given to me by good Christians, who are both for and against communicating with spirits, are these:

- Translations of the Old Testament of the Bible from the original Greek and Hebrew say we aren't allowed to call up or raise up the dead. Therefore, we aren't permitted to initiate the contact.

- The dead sleep until the Resurrection, therefore, they aren't able to come and visit us before then.

- The body and soul stay in the grave until the Resurrection.

- The devil and demons are the only ones who can communicate with physical beings, so all spirits communicating with us must be from Satan.

- The spirit could come from God or from Satan, so to be on the safe side, we need to stay away from all spirits who are communicating with us.

- There is the chance that we will open ourselves up to demonic entities and possible possession if we start to communicate with the dead.

• We don't want to offend God or go against His will or our Church.

If parents believe that the devil or demons are the only type of spirits that are spiritually able to communicate with us, they would understandably be frightened about these occurrences. Or if parents believe that communicating with good spirits is too dangerous because the result would definitely be demonic attachments, attacks or possession, that would be another reason to steer clear of opening up any doors to the dark side by allowing spirit communication.

Others are concerned because they don't want to go against what they perceive to be God's command prohibiting them from contacting even good spirits. They desire to be faithful to what they've interpreted to be God's final word on this matter. However, this particular Old Testament command has left some Christians feeling confused because they believe the spirit they are communicating with is their loved one, and the encounter has brought them enormous joy and peace. So they've torn and are looking for more answers and reassurances to resolve this conflict.

If any of the preceding describes your particular beliefs, but yet you have never personally researched the New Testament to learn if there is any information that exists that may give you a biblical green light to communicate with spirits and the way to do this safely, then your knee-jerk reaction will, of course, be a negative one. If fear and condemnation are your automatic shutdown responses to your child's confiding in you that he or she has seen a deceased loved one or a spirit, then this could have a harmful, lifelong effect on your child. Your child may be left feeling scared, guilty, perplexed, stigmatized, crazy, and alone. You are his or her whole world, and an infallible authority figure in your child's eyes. If the spiritual contacts continue on over the years, your child may feel further isolated, even from you, realizing they don't have anyone to turn to for support and guidance. I have even had adults contact me for guidance who have experienced spiritual gifts such as having telepathic communication from spirits, or seeing the spirit of their loved one, or having visions of future events, and they wondered whether they were going crazy or whether these were just figments of their imagination.

As your child grows into adulthood and if the gift stays with your child without your support, he or she may eventually turn away from your particular religious affiliation and beliefs and may later seek out other belief systems that are more compatible, nonjudgmental, and tolerant of your child's spiritual gifts.

But what if your interpretation, perceptions, and judgments may be mistaken? For those of you who believe that God would never allow spirit communication and are frightened or disturbed because your child sees spirits, I have some reassuring information to share with you, which may never have been pointed out to you before. For your children's sakes, I ask that you at least read and consider the following information, which is taken from the New Testament of the Bible about spirit communication. It just might help greatly alleviate some of your long-held fears and concerns about spiritual encounters you or your child is having.

For example, followers of Jesus Christ are expected to emulate Christ's life and teachings as their role model, as documented in the New Testament. They are also expected to follow the teachings of Christ's closest disciples that are written about in the Bible. So it is worth noting that the New Testament does not mention that Jesus or His apostles have condemned communicating with spirits. In fact, just the opposite. The Bible records that Jesus and His disciples talked to spirits themselves! The New Testament of the Bible actually instructs us on how to discern carefully a spirit that we are communicating with but doesn't prohibit or discourage it.

The Bible also shows that souls do not literally sleep after they die. As an example, the New Testament cites a story told by Jesus about spirits that have died and were having a conversation with each other in the afterlife. The story is the Rich Man, Lazarus, and

Abraham tale. In this narrative, the tormented Rich Man asks Abraham to send the beggar Lazarus back to earth from the afterlife to warn his rich brothers to repent their ways. Abraham, with Lazarus standing by his side, did not say that it was impossible for Lazarus to return to earth to give them a warning, but rather he said that the brothers would not repent even if someone rises from the dead to warn them.

This story can be read in full detail in Luke 16:19–31. But it indicates two things to me about spirits: (1) that the spirits of the Rich Man, Lazarus, and Abraham were *not literally* sleeping in the afterlife and were communicating with each other, and (2) that those who die realize that there is the possibility that spirits can be sent back to earth (rising from the dead) to communicate messages to human beings, if it were deemed to help.

The Bible also says that in the Last Days, the Holy Spirit will be giving more gifts. Many theologians and scholars today believe that the signs we are now seeing in our world are pointing to those literal Last Days.

For your reflection and consideration, in the following I have paraphrased some scriptures from the New Testament of the Bible I believe are accepting of the practice of spirit communication. The exact scriptural references are included for your convenience so that you can look them up in your own Bible.

- Jesus, while living on earth, communicated with the spirits of Moses and Elijah on Mt. Tabor in front of witnesses—His apostles Peter, James, and John. (Luke 9:28–36)

- Jesus said his followers would do greater things than the (miracle) works He did. (John 14:9–14)

- The Apostle Peter indicates that, in the Last Days, God said that He would pour out His Spirit on all people. Your sons and daughters will prophesy, your young men will see visions, your old men will dream dreams. (Acts 2:17–18)

- The Apostle Paul indicates that the prophets, whom Paul was counseling, were talking to spirits, and that those spirits were under the control of the prophets. Paul referenced the fact that God is not a God of disorder but of peace when it comes to spirits. (1 Corinthians 14:26–33)

- The Apostle Paul lists gifts of the Holy Spirit such as, discerning of spirits, wisdom, knowledge, faith, healing, miraculous powers, and prophecy. (1 Corinthians 12:3–11)

- The Apostle John did *not* condemn communicating with spirits, but rather gave us instructions on how to test spirits to discern whether they are from God and could be believed. (1 John 4:1–3)

So how does one then reconcile the prohibitions in the Old Testament about spirit communication vs. the practice in the New Testament in which Jesus and His disciples were talking to spirits? If you agree that the New Testament of the Bible supercedes the Old Testament of the Bible, as I do, and if you understand that the Apostle John was telling us how to test a spirit responsibly that we are communicating with (and didn't condemn the practice), then I believe this helps answer your question and you and your child's dilemma. Did you notice that the Apostle Paul listed discerning of spirits as one of the gifts of the Holy Spirit? If Paul is to be believed, when then would one have the need to discern a spirit? Why, when we are communicating with one, of course!

Another example of the New Testament superceding some commands in the Old Testament would be the "eye for an eye" command being replaced with Jesus saying to "forgive your brother seventy times seven." Therefore, do not the just-referenced New Testament scriptures about spirit communication also show a new way too?

Those of you who would like to encourage your spiritually gifted child, I agree, do have a valid reason to be apprehensive about opening up the door to demonic entities. However, I also believe that God provides a safe balancing act to allow spirit communication, while at the same time shielding your child. I do not believe that God would give one a spiritual gift for His Holy Purposes and would not also give us a way to protect ourselves when using this particular gift of the Holy Spirit. I believe the problem comes into play when we do not use all the necessary discerning and protective armor that God has provided.

To communicate safely with spirits and angels that are always around us but in another dimension, it is imperative that you at least test and discern spirits, angels, and other holy beings to be sure they are actually of God as advised in 1 John 4:1–3 and to go directly to Christ asking Him to protect you from spirits that are not from God.

For more detailed information on how parents can teach themselves and their children to discern spirits, to learn about different types of supernatural gifts and contacts and to learn about powerful prayers to protect them from spirits not of God, please read chapter 6 on this subject. This information will help you and your child feel spiritually armed and safe, while allowing you to nurture his or her gift from God's Holy Spirit for a higher divine purpose beyond your own human understanding. Remember to whom much is given, much is expected.

As always, though, your source for truth on all things is God. Ask Him to speak directly to your heart on these matters so that you can know how best to help your child the way that God is leading you to do. Please keep an open mind and heart and seek His direct guidance above all others.

If you do make the choice to embrace your child's spiritual gift (or your own), you don't have to leave your Christian faith to do so. If you have been hurt in the past by church members, family, or friends who have rejected or condemned your gift, please try to forgive them and let it go. They are probably very scared about spirits themselves and are worried about your welfare. Unless they have walked in your shoes, they cannot understand what it is like to have joyful and peaceful communication with those in the afterlife. You may want to consider searching for another church or denomination that may be more tolerant of your gift.

To protect yourself or your child from negative judgments or opposition from others, you may want to keep those gifts close to the vest. Only share them with people who you trust and who you feel will be okay with it.

If you sincerely believe that God has gifted you or your child this way, ask for God's strength, courage, and guidance on how to use this gift properly. A gift from God is always meant for a higher good and purpose. Therefore, humbly ask to be in service to Him and ask how you can best utilize any spiritual gift you have been given. Being in service to God can be a tough road with many obstacles, as you may have already discovered. Talk to your child about his or her gift and explain that it is best used if he or she asks to be in service to God with it.

CHAPTER 6

Children's Spiritual Gifts, Angels and Demons, and Protective Prayers

This book is filled with so many heartwarming and uplifting children's stories of afterlife contacts you may feel that some sections of this chapter on evil entities may seem completely out of place, extremely fear mongering, or unnecessarily alarmist. It is precisely because I greatly desire for all your children's experiences to continue to be wonderful that I feel it is crucial to share the flip side of spirit communication with you. I am trying to shed light on the often-overlooked darker side of spirit communication for three main reasons: First, this book is also about nurturing your children's spiritual gifts and protecting them. Second, it answers a number of questions that I have been frequently asked about over the years. Third, as a teacher of afterlife contacts and signs, I feel it would be grossly negligent of me to ignore the unpleasant dark side and to give you only half of the picture and information.

Since I have had some painful learning lessons in this particular area, I hope to keep you from all the potential pitfalls and land mines that can accompany spiritual gifts. Knowledge is power. So please read this chapter with an open mind and heart. It is with experience, love, concern, and caring that I share this additional knowledge with you in order to protect your children who communicate with spirits and wish to continue to do so safely.

Do Satan and Demons Exist?

A 2007 Harris Poll reports that 62 percent of the public believes in the existence of the devil (Satan/Lucifer/powerful leader of the banished and fallen demonic angels from Heaven). Even though a majority of the public believes in the reality of the devil and his demonic followers, there is a popular notion that these evil entities really do not exist. It bears repeating that one of the greatest French poets of the nineteenth century Charles Baudelaire is known for having said that the devil's greatest trick is to persuade us that he does not exist. I believe the same is true today in our twenty-first century just as it was back in the nineteenth.

Now what could possibly happen if you do not believe in evil entities? Well, then you would not bother to protect your children properly, and that is how you can unknowingly and involuntarily open up the door to the dark side and to dark experiences.

Anyone who has personally encountered these evil and destructive forces, such as priests and ministers who have performed exorcisms and who have spiritually cleansed houses, or laypeople who have investigated disturbing or violent paranormal hauntings, or those who have had out-of-body or near-death experiences (NDE's) into the demonic realms, will vehemently disagree with the notion that Satan and evil entities do not exist. Those who are directly involved and experienced in spiritual warfare understand this best. There is a very interesting show on the Investigation Discovery Channel called *A Haunting*, which reenacts true accounts of these types of paranormal encounters. The true accounts in this program are on the more extreme side, but the point I am trying to make is that they are eye-openers for anyone who does not believe that evil entities exist. I recommend that you watch a few of these episodes and reflect on them as they may help give you a new awareness.

When you think about it, does everything not have an opposite: positive or negative, hot or cold, beautiful or ugly, love or hate, and good or evil? I am not advocating that you fearfully dwell or obsess about the devil or demon spirits because they may benefit from feeding on your fears. Rather, I would like you to be aware that you can and should protect yourself and your children from these entities by calling directly on the God-Christ, your Creator, your Divine Source, or your Higher Power. You do not want to be playing Russian roulette with your children's safety. You do not want to leave them vulnerable by automatically assuming that the entity communicating with your child (or you) is a good one and is of God just because it says so or looks or sounds nice.

I have personally learned and have found out the hard way that demons will try to trick you into believing that they are the "good guys," your departed loved ones, lost little children or adults, spirit guides, angels, Jesus, or other holy beings—when they are not who they say they are. These evil entities can and will lie to you from the spiritual realms, just as human beings who live on the physical realms on earth can lie to you. These entities are very clever and extremely experienced at doing this. They will try to gain your trust for unsavory purposes and can cause you a great deal of confusion and distress. So it is imperative that you and your children stay one step ahead of these spirits by testing and clearing *all* spirits and asking for God's holy protection, which I will go into in more detail in this chapter.

Protecting Young Children

Our departed loved ones are sent to us by God for a variety of reasons:

1. To let us know that they are okay.

2. To make it clear that they still see and hear us,

3. To let us know that an afterlife does exist.

4. To help us heal from grief.

5. To bring us love and comfort.

6. To protect us.

7. To guide us in our lives.

There are other important reasons known only to God.

Because very young children are so pure, usually you will not need to fear for their safety when it comes to what types of spirits will be communicating with them. God assigns His mighty angels to watch over these pure innocents to keep them safe from harm in this regard. However, every now and then a malevolent entity will seem to fly under the radar and will communicate with or scare a child. The reason is that denser darker entities are closer to the earth's realms than God's angels of light are. Malevolent entities can even spiritually project themselves to look like monster creatures, spiders, or attacking animals, to name a few of the unpleasant ways they will manifest themselves. The malevolent spirit's endgame may be to try to scare the child away from his or her God-given spiritual gift.

To empower your children to handle scary spirits bothering them (as well as yourself), please teach them that if they are ever frightened by anything, to pray immediately to God for help. They can simply say out loud, "Help me, God, or Jesus" or say whatever name you refer to your Creator or Divine Source. Your children will get to witness firsthand how calling out to Almighty God will chase away the undesirable or scary spirit. They may even be privileged at times to see the angels flying in on their behalf to chase out those spirits. This will start to internalize some important messages to your children. Namely, that they are not alone, that they are not powerless, and that God heard their prayers and will protect them. The result will be that your children will have a feeling of empowerment and control over the supernatural circumstances going on around them and that they need not be afraid of them.

As children get to be around five years of age, it would be helpful for them to get in the habit of saying a quick prayer to God or Jesus for protection whenever they sense a spirit's presence. If the spirit is of God, the spirit will stay and you will have a feeling of peace when in its presence. Any spirits not of God, however, will be forced to leave. I have discovered that God will send His warring angels to force them to leave if they try to stay.

Different Types of Spiritual Gifts and Contacts

The children's stories in this book mainly involve seeing and hearing spirits and their telepathic thoughts. Additionally, it is possible to sense a spirit's emotions. You may smell a strong familiar scent that connects you to them when they are around. You may feel how the person passed over. It is also possible for a spirit to take over one's very limp hand and write messages with it, if you are so willing—although this gift usually happens to adults.

Dreams

Spirits often visit us in our dreams to communicate with us. Since different types of spirits—the good and the not so good—can easily visit us in our dreams, please teach your children when they are old enough to pray, to ask God, their Creator, Divine Source, or Jesus for His protection before they go to sleep. I encourage you to have this be a part of their daily routine before going to bed. The same is just as important for adults to do.

Since God sends our loved ones to us to bring us comfort, if the dream of a loved one causes you or your child to feel distress, this would not be an authentic spiritual visit from your loved one. Because we want the true spirits of our loved ones to visit us in our dreams and to bring us the love and comfort that God desires for us to have, the bedtime prayers of protection will greatly help in this regard. The prayers will also help with reducing nightmares. (Keeping children away from watching violent or disturbing movies and reading scary books before bedtime can also help reduce nightmares.)

Children may feel scared at bedtime because they may actually be seeing frightening spirits in the room from time to time. Children who feel scared will feel safer if they take a religious article to bed with them and if they are taught to pray to God to protect them. Leaving on a soft low light in the room can help a child who feels afraid.

Adults' Dreams of Loved Ones

Since I am on the topic of dreams, I want to include a common problem that adults often consult me about. As your children get older, they may also experience these same types of episodes. Over the years, many adults have asked me what to do to stop hurtful and disturbing dreams of their deceased loved ones. In their upsetting dreams, the spirits would appear looking and sounding like their loved ones, but the disturbing dream scenario would be along these lines: their loved ones may have been angry at them, been mean to them, ignored them, rejected them, seemed lost, seemed sickly, seemed in pain, or seemed to be bleeding, or their spouses or significant others were being extremely affectionate to other people right in front of them.

Since God sends our loved ones to us for the purpose of bestowing comfort and peace, even though the spirits may have looked like their loved ones, if the spirits' visits were not giving them peace and comfort, then they would not be the true spirits of their loved ones sent by God. I refer to these spirits as "imposter spirits" (demons). Posing as a loved one is a trick it will often pull to exploit your vulnerabilities when you are grieving. Don't let the spirit succeed by buying into the notion that this was your actual loved one. Reject it and do not believe it.

When I have advised a grieving person bothered by these types of dreams to say a prayer faithfully to God or Jesus every night before going to bed and to ask for His holy protection and for Him to rebuke and bind spirits not in service to Him (Satan and his demons), they would later report back to me that their bad dreams were rare now. They were finally being replaced with comforting dreams of their loved ones.

Once you get into the practice of saying protective prayers before going to bed, you may find that in the very middle of your bad dream, you will have the presence of mind to ask the spirit if it is of God. You may also find yourself automatically calling on God or Jesus for His protection right in the middle of your nightmare. You will be amazed at how quickly the unwanted spirit will leave your dream if you do these things! You will also be surprised to find out that when you directly ask a suspicious spirit in your dream if it is of God, it will actually admit its deception by saying no if it is not, and then it will disappear! This is because spirits have to answer truthfully when they are asked this direct question.

As your child gets older, please explain about these imposter spirits who may try to communicate with them in their dreams and in their awakened state. You will be helping to save them from the distress that these negative spirits often bring.

A "Knowingness" or Intuition, Premonitions, Prophecies, and Precognitive Dreams and Visions

Spiritual gifts appear in many ways. Your child may have a strong knowingness or intuition through a sense, feeling, or vision about a particular situation. For instance, a child may tell you that his or her grandfather has just died. Some children and adults may have premonitions and experience a gut feeling or uneasiness giving them warnings about a future event.

Some people make prophecies. They predict events deemed to be divinely inspired. Other people have precognitive visions and dreams about future events or situations. Some have reported seeing a glowing purple and green ball of light, which was a portal through which their visions came. Sometimes visions and dreams of future events may indeed become a reality; other times, they may not. It would be useful to record in a journal all visions and dreams that seem vivid and important for future reference. It may be best to take a wait-

and-see attitude before automatically assuming that all advanced knowledge is accurate. The reason is that not all future knowledge comes from spirits of God. Even if a future event shown to you does come from God, the timing may end up being a lot different from the original timing you were shown. It may not come about until years later.

You may want to see if the future events shown to you are repeated about three times in dreams or visions as another indicator as to whether the information you are receiving is reliable. When future events start to unfold before you, try to remember to take a moment to ask for God's protection. Afterward, please ask for God's guidance and clarification before taking any action on future knowledge.

If your child is being given unsettling information about future events that you or your child has no control over and could not have possibly changed the outcome, then pray for the people involved. Your prayers are very important, and they will help sustain them. Please be sure that your child knows that he or she was *not* responsible for causing anything to happen that they were given advanced knowledge of. It is my belief that God is the One who has the power to intervene to change a particular situation from occurring, and that everything is in God's omnipotent hands. In the end, God turns every tragedy around for a greater spiritual good even if we are not able to recognize that right now. Someday we will.

If you find this particular gift to be too difficult for your child, then please advise your child that he or she can talk to God about removing it. If some children do want to continue with this gift, let them know that they should ask God to guide them to be in service to Him to help others in a meaningful way.

Meditation and Prayer

Meditation and prayer are our spiritual links and direct lifelines to God. When we take the time to meditate, this quiet time gives God an opportunity to talk to us because our souls are more open to receiving then. When we enter a meditative state of consciousness, we are also wide-open vessels for all types of spirits to come through to us, similar to when we are in the REM, or rapid eye movement, state of sleep. So before you do go into a meditative state, it is important to ask out loud for God, your Divine Source, or Jesus (the God-Christ) to protect you from spirits that are not of God. Repeat your prayers of protection at frequent intervals during this relaxed state of consciousness.

Spirits' Activities

Good Paranormal Happenings

Good spirits and angels who visually appear to children or adults also have the capability of doing some unusual physical things, such as moving objects, touching us, speaking to us, playing with computers, playing with electrical devices, having the bed push down if they are lying beside us, and so on. They usually do these things while remaining invisible. I have identified in greater detail the twenty common and good paranormal types of ADCs, which include the six just mentioned, in my book *God's Gift of Love: After-Death Communications* that our departed loved ones so often do to let us know they are around us. Our loved ones' afterlife signs are meant to bring us comfort from them and God.

Because many people are not aware that spirits of our loved ones, angels, and pets often communicate with us by using at least those twenty common types of contacts, one may understandably be wary and left feeling a little unnerved by a paranormal contact when the visit was only meant to bring you comfort.

The first time an adult or an older child sees or senses a spirit, it is normal and natural to feel a little nervous, especially if that person is not asking for any contact. If you have the presence of mind to ask for God, your Divine Source, or Jesus's (the God-Christ) holy protection when a spirit appears to you, you will feel completely protected and have the peace you desire during this supernatural occur-rence. A good spirit sent by God will leave when you ask it to be-cause they do not want to cause you any distress. They may opt instead to come in your dreams in the future so as not to frighten you. If you want good spirits to stay, while at the same time desiring to remove any evil spirits in the room, then call on God or Jesus (the God-Christ) and ask for His holy protection and for him to bind and rebuke all spirits not in service to Him. You will then feel at peace and be able to relax and enjoy the visit. If you find that you are enjoying these communications, please acknowledge your grateful-ness to God and to them for the visit.

Bad Paranormal Happenings

The difference between a good spirit's physical contacts and a bad spirit's physical contacts is that a bad spirit (demon) will do some-thing scary, menacing, destructive, harmful, or evil. It may even shake your bed uncontrollably. It may throw things in the room. It may physically attack you. If you have a gift to be able to see spirits, demons may manifest themselves as ugly crawling bugs or some other fear-provoking creature. You may feel like you are being ha-rassed or feel threatened. You may sense a heavy and dark energy presence around you even if nothing physically is happening to frighten you. A demon spirit may look like an ordinary spirit, but the difference is that it may act angry, lost, scared, and confused. It may appear to be bleeding or to be in need of your help. Please do not fall for these tactics. Spirits in Heaven are not angry, scared, or lost. They do not bleed. There is no confusion in the spiritual realms. Every spirit who crosses over has angels, provided by God, who lead them to where they are supposed to go.

You may find that if you ask, demand, or yell at even a nice-looking demon spirit to go away, it usually won't honor your request, so you may be left feeling powerless, vulnerable, and scared. In all these sit-uations, tell your children to call out loud directly on God, your Di-vine Source, or Jesus (the God-Christ) to rebuke and bind the spirit for you and to ask for God's holy protection. There'll be a noticeable change in the room if you do.

Hauntings

If you find that even your prayers to the God-Christ or your Creator are not stopping what seems to you or your child to be an evil, disturbing, destructive, angry, threatening, or relentless spirit haunting you or your dwelling, then please contact your clergy or those whose ministry is to cleanse demons from dwellings and people. Those involved in spiritual warfare know how to do this safely.

Protection for Older Children with Spiritual Gifts

If you embrace and nurture your child's spiritual gift and if both you and your child are open to this gift, your child may be blessed by God to be able to communicate with spirits throughout his or her whole lifetime. In that case, more knowledge is needed when it comes to discerning good and bad spirits. They will need to know how to test, chase away, rebuke, bind, or expose any unwanted, malevolent, or imposter spirits that may be around and that may be trying to fool or take advantage of your child (or you). If you ignore them, they may start to interfere with your child's ability to communicate clearly with good spirits. They may start to give mixed, confusing, and distracting messages. They may steal your child's sense of peace from him or her. You do not want your older child or teenager to inadvertently crack open the door to the dark side by not bothering to test the spirit and by not asking directly for God, your Divine Source, or Jesus's (the God-Christ) holy protection, therefore allowing any malevolent spirits to hang around.

An analogy would be to imagine yourself being a police officer standing guard outside of your home. You have been informed that there are imposters in the neighborhood who look like the good guys, friends or family. People have been tricked into letting these imposters into their homes. So with that background information, as the police guard of your home, some people approach you and ask to enter your home. These people tell you they are good people, or friends, or family members of yours. You can't be sure if they are being honest with you or just wearing a clever disguise. So you submit them to a test to find out if they are who they say they are. If they pass, they have earned a one-event security clearance and will be allowed to enter into your home. The analogy I am presenting to you is similar to the type of test under "Three Steps for Protection" (see pp. 197–198) I strongly recommend that you follow these steps each time any spirit wants to communicate with you. Again, please believe me, it would never be my intention to frighten anyone. I believe that knowledge is power, and this knowledge can give you an enlightened heads-up, remove your fears, and protect and empower you if you know what to do.

Asking to be surrounded with the white light of God or calling on angels for your protection are all good things to do; however, I have learned in my spiritual work that this is not always powerful enough. I have found that *the* most powerful and effective way to protect yourself is to go directly to the God-Christ asking for His Almighty protection, and to use the Three Steps for Protection method. I have personally found this to be the gold standard of protection.

When your child goes directly to the God-Christ for protection, He will send specific angels in service to Him trained for this special purpose. God is omniscient, so He knows which of His angels are the best ones to protect you. By going directly to the God-Christ, your child will be helped to feel a direct and personal connection to God. It will enable your child to experience His tender, loving care.

Essential Steps for Protection

If your older child has a strong gift that continues and stays with him, then the three important steps, when used together, will prove repeatedly to be extremely powerful and effective when it comes to distinguishing and removing spirits that are not from God's holy realms. This valuable information was given to Sunni Welles by her angels of God. Welles is the author of the extraordinary enlightening spiritual and prophetic book *Glimpses of Heaven from the Angels Who Live There.* She is also a close and trusted friend of mine. These three steps are knowledge that the angels said God wanted them to share with everyone. From the feedback I have received from others and from my own personal experiences, these steps are enormously effective and powerful.

Because everyone does not have the same belief system, I am also going to be offering another choice of steps for you to follow in the next section, which I hope will ring true to you with regard to your own personal belief system.

Three Steps for Protection—Christians

As mentioned earlier, approximately 82 percent of Americans told Gallup interviewers in 2007 that they identified with a Christian religion. Thus, the three essential steps from the angels and the specific faith-based terminology will especially resonate with those in this group, but it is also recommended for anyone of any faith or belief system who feels an inner guidance to do so. However, if these steps are not compatible with your own belief system and if you do not feel comfortable using them, then there are other more universal protection steps (see pp. 199–200) that I have provided for your use in another section in this chapter titled "Three Universal Steps for Protection."

The three essential steps to share with your older children with Christian beliefs are:

1. *Confessing of sins*—It is very important to confess one's sins before beginning one's spiritual work to prepare and cleanse oneself adequately to be a pure vessel for the Holy Spirit to work through. (Purity = more protection and attracts more angelic spirits of God.)

2. *Rebuking the spirit, and Christ's protection*—Pray out loud or under your breath directly to Jesus (the God-Christ) asking Him to bind and rebuke Satan and all his followers, beings, entities, and spirits that are around that are not committed and not in service to Christ. Then ask for the full armor of Christ's protection. Teach your child to do this before he allows a spirit to communicate with him and repeat the prayers at frequent intervals while communicating with a spirit. Why repeat it? Because spirits who are bound and rebuked may only be temporarily removed from our presence.

3. *Test and clear the spirit (security clearance)*—Teach your child to ask the spirit these two specific questions: "Do you acknowledge that Jesus Christ has come in the flesh?" (Note: this is a directive for testing the spirits for discernment in 1 John 4:1–3), and also ask the spirit, "Are you committed and in service to Our Lord and Savior Jesus Christ?" They must give you a yes answer to this direct question. Negative spirits are unable to avoid or lie about being in service to Christ. The result of these direct questions when said together will out or expose the spirits not of God and not in service to Christ.

Following all three steps is extremely important to have the maximum amount of protection from God as well as being able to distinguish properly whether the spirit is from God's holy realms or the dark side. According to Welles's angels in *Glimpses of Heaven,* if some amount of time elapses after you first cleared and tested the spirit, and the information is coming through, you will need to repeat steps 2 and 3. Why? Because imposter spirits can return later when your guard is down, and they will try to fly under the radar. If they do, then it is possible that false messages may start to be given. So if some time has gone by during your child's initial testing, have them repeat the protective prayers and clear and test the spirit again (steps

2 and 3). They should do this at frequent intervals during the communication to be on the safe side.

A word of caution: Even after doing the three steps just discussed, if you perceive that any messages given to your child are "evil" or make you feel uncomfortable or contradict scriptural doctrine, your antenna should go up. Stop the communication immediately and do the protective prayers, following the rebuking, testing, and clearing steps again. Analyzing the content of the information you are receiving is another way to discern whether the spirit was truly sent by God. There are malevolent, imposter spirits (demons) that pretend to be good spirits, our loved ones, angels, spirit guides, Jesus, and other holy beings. They do this for the purposes of giving false messages, causing spiritual confusion, causing errors in doctrine, or wanting just to inflict emotional pain, grief, or discord.

As I previously mentioned, I personally know about imposter spirits (demons) because I have encountered them. When I used the protective prayers and testing and clearing methods, these spirits exposed their true dark nature, even though they presented themselves at first to be from God's holy realms. To illustrate this point, the Bible states that even Satan can disguise himself as an angel of light (2 Corinthians 11:14).

I am aware that the preceding steps are time consuming. Your older child will be tempted to skip over them. However, if God's Holy Spirit has given your child a gift to communicate with spirits, he or she will need to be responsible and use all these resources to keep from being taken advantage of. It will be well worth the time and effort. Your child will have the reward of feeling comfortable that the spirit doing the communicating is from God's holy realms and that the information he or she is receiving from the spirit is trustworthy. Over time, with practice, your child will be able to fly quickly through these steps.

Three Universal Steps for Protection

For those of other spiritual or religious belief systems, the just-discussed three steps will still work very effectively for you too. However, if you feel uncomfortable with the terminology in those steps or if it goes against your personal belief system, then please use the following universal steps instead for your older children's protection when communicating with spirits:

1. *Cleansing*—It is very important to state one's wrongdoings to God, your Creator, or Divine Source before beginning one's spiritual work to prepare and cleanse oneself adequately to be a pure vessel for God's Holy Spirit to work with. (Purity = more protection and attracts more angelic spirits of God.)

2. *God's holy protection*—Teach your older child to ask out loud or under his breath for God's holy protection from spirits that are not in service to Him, before your child allows the spirit to communicate.

3. *Testing the spirit (security clearance)*—Ask the spirit directly if it is of God and if it is in service to God. (Be sure you get a direct yes answer here.)

Please teach your children to do steps 2 and 3 at frequent intervals during the spiritual contact because spirits not of God may only be temporarily removed from our presence. If your children repeat steps 2 and 3 during the course of their communication, they will be less vulnerable to being taken advantage of by spirits that pretend to be from God's holy realms when they are not. If they know the children are unsuspecting of their true dark nature and motives, they will run with it and will enjoy giving them untruthful and mixed messages that can be harmful and confusing. This happens many more times than people realize.

Protection Prayers Are Empowering

You now have the essential information you need to protect and guide your children throughout their whole lives when it comes to using their God-given spiritual gifts safely and responsibly when communicating with spirits. This information will serve them (and you) well if they faithfully follow it. The simple one-line prayers will help give your younger children peace and a feeling of security. The more detailed and in-depth protective steps mentioned will help them when they are teenagers and adults. These protective prayers will help take away their fears and their feelings of helplessness. This result will empower them knowing that if they call on God or Jesus (the God-Christ),they will get His immediate heavenly protection, and those bothersome spirits will be driven away. Their fears will vanish, and they will feel God's peace instead. This will help them to feel more enthusiastic about utilizing the gift that God has given them for a greater good and for His holy purposes.

Do Children Have to Do Anything to Strengthen Their Gifts?

While it is always recommended that you quiet yourself, relax, pray, and meditate, when God gives a gift from His Holy Spirit, your child will not have to do anything special to strengthen his or her gift. If God wants to strengthen it for His own purposes, He will. It is all in God's omnipotent hands. The most important question people need to ask themselves is this, Do I really want to be in service to God with my gift for God's purposes and not for my own glory? If so, they need to let God know this and be open and humble to following God's lead. Then utilizing those three essential protection steps will provide them with a spiritual security blanket throughout their lives.

PART IV

Life's Most Profound Questions

CHAPTER 7

The Circle of Life, Near-Death Experiences, and Glimpses of Heaven

As children, many of us have assumed, or have been taught to believe, that the Circle of Life for our souls happens in this particular sequence of events: Our first existence begins when we are born on earth. We live. We die. Then, it is hoped that we will go to a heavenly afterlife.

Yet even though we may have been taught that particular order of events, some who have had NDEs have found there to be a different order of events concerning our soul's creation. Their experiences and conversations in the spiritual realms convinced them that God created us first as souls that lived in Heaven with Him *before* we came down to earth in physical bodies for important learning lessons. Additionally, there are even some stories in this book in which children have remembered being in Heaven and talking with deceased family members while they were waiting to come to earth to be born. The family members they had remembered talking to in Heaven had actually *died before the children were ever born*, and their souls palled around together coexisting for a time in Heaven. Therefore, the Circle of Life for our souls could actually be considered to be in this particular order of events: Heaven, earth, death, and afterlife. (For those of you who may be concerned about this from a religious perspective, I don't believe that this spiritual concept conflicts with the belief that the first humans on earth were Adam and Eve in the Garden of Eden.)

When it comes to Heaven, there are three kinds of people: those who definitely believe in its existence, those who want to believe in its existence, and those who don't believe at all.

Whether or not you believe the soul was first created and lived in Heaven with God, if you are reading this book, then you most likely want to believe or do believe there is a Heaven. Now even if you firmly do believe there is a heavenly afterlife awaiting you, Heaven may seem mysterious and a bit scary because of the lack of specific details generally known. Your idea of Heaven may be that you just float around on a cloud playing on a harp all day, as is often portrayed in movies. Even believing that Heaven does exist requires a significant amount of faith and trust in God in conjunction with sacred and revered books and teachings, in order to have that confidence. Unless you have been visited by a departed loved one from beyond or you have been privileged to have personally visited the afterlife through an NDE, through dreams, or through an out-of-body experience, you may have gnawing doubts and trepidation about the unknown aspects of the afterlife.

Not wanting to separate from our loved ones, the basic human instinct to live and the fear of the unknown can instill a strong personal desire to stay here on earth with our families and friends for as long as humanly possible, where life is familiar and may seem safer even if imperfect. Most feel that it's is a real tragedy to die believing that the departed adult, teenager, child, or baby has missed out on so many wonderful future experiences on earth. And, of course, it's a painful personal tragedy for those left behind who miss and love the departed cherished person in their lives. Most won't talk about this taboo topic or adequately prepare themselves or their children for death until someone close to them dies or is about to die.

Our modern-day society tends to shy away from this uncomfortable and painful topic like the plague. If someone tries openly to discuss his or her own impending death, we may even find ourselves immediately shutting down the conversation saying "Oh, don't talk that way," superstitiously hoping that if we don't discuss their death, we won't jinx them, and it just won't happen. Yet in reality, *nobody gets out of here alive* even if we wish we could stay here forever.

Little-Known Details About the Afterlife

Happily, I would like to share with you some very exciting and specific details about the afterlife that you may never have come across before. This information may take away your own personal fear of death and the afterlife and may help you feel more comfortable discussing these topics with your children and with others. It may even help you look forward to the afterlife! What a concept! So please take a slow, deep breath, say a little prayer to God, if you will, and ask God to open up your mind and heart to be able to determine the truth of the information that I believe He is leading me to share with you.

Those Who Have "Died" and Lived to Tell About It

Thankfully for us, there are people who have been privileged to get a glimpse into Heaven and the afterlife when they had a NDE. There are many books on NDEs written by well-respected doctors, researchers, and people who have had the actual NDE.

From the myriad of NDEs I have read over the years, their breathtaking sneak previews into Heaven have given us something extremely glorious, exciting, and hopeful to look forward to.

Many who left their physical bodies for a short period have explained that they were quite surprised that they felt an instant peace, calm, and warmth immediately after their spirits separated from their human bodies. They realized that they felt no connection to their physical bodies if they had a chance to view their bodies from above them. They no longer had any physical pain. They were able to fly freely and unencumbered and were able to communicate through thought with others in the spiritual realms. Some discovered (and many on earth believe) that we are spiritual beings having a human experience in our mortal bodies while we are "temporarily" living on earth for important lessons learned for our souls' spiritual growth.

Some described being met by an incredibly magnificent being of radiant light and unconditional love that they called God or Jesus. Some described being met by and reunited with departed loved ones, pets, angels, and other holy beings. Some saw cities, dwelling places or houses, churches, prayer centers, roads, lovely gardens with flowers of vibrant colors, meadows with lush grass, brooks, streams, oceans, rivers, mountains, hills, fantastic skies, and sunsets. Some children have reported hearing an enormous playground full of kids who were laughing and playing. In other words, Heaven was a lot like earth in many ways, only Heaven was glorious beyond all earthly imagination. The love they felt there was a million times more powerful than anything they had ever experienced on earth. Their celebratory feelings of awe, joy, and love were overwhelming. Most, who have had NDEs, no longer feared death because of their personal journeys into the afterlife. Many who were told that they had to go back to earth because it was not yet their time were very disappointed and wanted to stay there!

In Dr. Melvin Morse's *New York Times* best-selling book *Closer to the Light,* children who had NDEs talked about seeing Jesus, angels, a bright light at the end of a tunnel, rainbows, and beautiful flowers; running through fields with God; getting to double-jump rope in Heaven; and seeing souls waiting to be born. It was a place full of cheer and bright light.

In Dr. Raymond A. Moody, Jr.'s best-selling book, *Life After Life,* his research and interviews show that some, who had NDEs, were able to view their physical bodies while being above them. Some had the experience of being pulled through a dark tunnel; others saw family and friends who had passed over before them. Some came into the presence of an incredibly brilliant being of light and love that was a personal being. When in the presence of this being of light, there was a pure transfer of thoughts between them. The being of light showed the spirit a panoramic view of its life on earth.

In 1973 Betty Eadie was pronounced dead after having routine surgery. In her amazing *New York Times* best-selling book, *Embraced by the Light,* Eadie describes her NDE. In the book, to paraphrase, Eadie tells of being automatically pulled into a tunnel; being met by her angels, spirits, and Jesus; and feeling an explosion of love filling her when she came into Jesus's presence and light. She knew she had finally come home, and her memory of Heaven was restored. Eadie saw beautiful mountains, valleys, oceans, gardens, and other universes. Compassion and love flowed into her from caring spirits around her when she had her difficult life's review. She found that spirits in Heaven had very joyful and meaningful work to do and were in service to God.

During Eadie's ethereal experience, she was able to view earth and its ongoing events. She learned that we were all actually created by God as spirits *first* living in Heaven *before* we came down to earth to live in our mortal bodies! Eadie discovered that we had courageously volunteered for specific missions, hardships, handicaps, and illnesses on earth because we knew there would be a great deal of spiritual growth and good to come out of those missions. She saw spirits choosing their own parents. She discovered that most of us knew ahead of time how we were going to die. Some made spiritual contracts with God to die as an infant for a higher purpose for the benefit of those around them. We knew that our lives on earth, no matter how short, were a gift from God and would help attain needed qualities for growth. Even so, when Eadie was told she had to go back and finish her mission on earth, she begged to stay. (What Eadie learned helps to answer the age-old question, "Why do bad things happen to good people?")

In 1989, Rev. Don Piper, an ordained minister, was pronounced dead after a horrible automobile accident. In his *New York Times* best-selling book, *90 Minutes in Heaven,* he explains how he found himself in Heaven and being met and embraced by a joyful, celebratory crowd of people, including loved ones and friends who had died before him. They all looked radiant. He had never felt so completely alive, loved, or happy. The continuous praise music he heard being sung to God was indescribably beautiful. He felt as if he had become one with the music. He saw pearly gates and streets that were actually paved in gold. He never felt the existence of time. Piper said it was because of the fervent prayers of many others that he was returned to life after being dead for ninety minutes. The overwhelming joy and unconditional love Piper felt while being in Heaven has had the effect of his constant yearning for the day he can return permanently to that glorious place again.

In 1985 Howard Storm, while waiting for an emergency operation in a Paris hospital, had an NDE. Howard has written about his riveting NDE in his book *My Descent into Death*. Prior to his NDE, Storm was an avowed atheist, not believing in God or an afterlife. Storm humbly acknowledges that as an atheist he lived his life as a rather unpleasant and angry human being. During his NDE his initial experience was a horrifying exception to the many other blissful NDEs reported. His negative ethereal experience was very disturbing to read about at first. However, in the midst of his despair and torment from the hideous, torturous creatures he encountered in the dark realm where he was stuck, he heard a voice within him telling him to pray to God. Even though Storm didn't believe there was a God, he followed the voice's advice to pray to God anyway. Storm then recalled a childhood singsong about Jesus loving him, and he passionately cried out to Jesus to save him. Mercifully after his plea to Jesus, his prayers were answered.

Jesus Himself came to him as an incredible being of light and love and tenderly lifted Storm out of that hellish realm. He was taken to a heavenly realm full of unconditional love, compassion, and ecstasy. Storm was able to view earth from Heaven's spiritual vantage point. After receiving spiritual answers to his many questions from a being Storm identifies as Jesus Christ and from the angels, Storm was told he needed to return to the world. Storm protested that he didn't want to leave Heaven! He was told to spread love back on earth. This was such a transformational experience for Storm that he eventually became an ordained minister and pastor.

Eadie, Piper, and Storm all found Heaven to be full of indescribable love permeating their whole beings. Heaven was so wonderful that they never wanted to leave, and all are longing for the day their earthly missions are over so that they can return forever. Their natural fear of death is gone. Their time in Heaven had profound life-changing effects on them. One reason why God may have allowed these NDEs to occur is that He may have wanted to grant more revelations and insights into the wonders and rewards of Heaven that are waiting for us. Knowing more specifics would naturally help us look forward to it instead of fearing it and God. Beam me up, Jesus!

The Circle of Life

If you believe, as I now do after my many years of spiritual research, that we were originally created as spirit/souls in Heaven before we came down to earth for a specific purpose, then the following blueprint and order of the Circle of Life will give you the basic knowledge you need to begin your talk with your child about death, the afterlife, and other profound spiritual matters. Perhaps this following scripture will help the religious who may be grappling with this new concept that I am laying out. "For he chose us in him *before the creation of the world* to be holy and blameless in his sight." Ephesians 1:4

I am only going to be discussing our return to Heaven. All other ethereal realms will have to be supplied by you at the appropriate age for your child, in accordance with your own personal belief system.

The blueprint of the Circle of Life I am going to be using will be in this sequence: heaven, earth, death, and heaven. These are the fundamental building blocks:

1. We were originally created as eternal spiritual beings by God and lived with God in Heaven.

2. We each volunteered to come to earth and made a plan with God to live in a mortal body temporarily for the purposes of our or others' soul growth to become closer to God and for other important spiritual reasons.

3. We stay on earth till our lessons and missions are completed unless God decides otherwise.

4. We stay until our mortal bodies die.

5. We die and our spirits separate from our physical bodies immediately.

6. We return to God with our spiritual bodies.

Let's turn to the next chapter where you'll find simplified explanations to give your children about some of life's most important, complex, and profound spiritual questions.

CHAPTER 8

Explaining Death, Grief, Heaven, God, Angels, Spirits, Afterlife Visits, and Our Life's Purpose

Why are we here? Seeing the bigger picture about the meaning of our lives will assist you in making more sense out of why we are here. It will be an invaluable resource in answering your children's questions about life, death, and Heaven. The information presented here is not meant to be a substitute for your own religious and spiritual beliefs for why we are here and for what gets us safely and soundly into Heaven. Even though there are essential spiritual reasons taught by major religions on this topic, I am not going to be discussing them. I will leave that up to you to discuss with your children in accordance with your own belief system. This book is meant to be inclusive and not about religious conversion. This chapter is offered as a spiritual supplement for you to consider and possibly embrace if it rings true to you. It may help fill in some important gaps about life and death that you have been wondering about. As I mentioned earlier, it also helps to give meaningful answers to the universal question, why do bad things happen to good people?

As with all other information given to you in this book, please pray to God to guide you to know the truth of what is being presented to you. Let God be your Spiritual Guide.

The Purpose of Coming to Earth

Even children eventually want to know why they are here. They may wonder why we would ever want to leave a great place like Heaven to come to earth, where there is pain, suffering, tears, and death. Here are some childlike explanations that you can use if this question arises.

You can explain that even though as spirits/souls we loved living in Heaven with God, where He first created us, many of us desired to come to earth for a little while to learn more and to grow spiritually stronger and even closer to God. Living on earth was the best way to do this. Earth is like a gigantic school, and we wanted to experience other things here that we couldn't in Heaven where everything is perfect. Living on earth where there are problems and hardships provides opportunities for faster growth of our souls. The reward for successfully completing these challenging learning lessons and missions on earth is getting to move up to higher heavenly realms/levels when we go back to Heaven. Each higher heavenly realm is even better than the one below it. Successfully completing our missions can eventually help us become more like God's angels and be as close to God as we can be. This is what each soul desires in its heart of hearts.

Before we came to earth, God made a special plan for each of us to follow about what we were going to learn here, what we were going to do to benefit our souls, what we could do to help other people, and what we could do to grow closer to Him in Heaven for all eternity. We were eager to come to earth for those reasons, and we volunteered for specific missions in the hopes that we would successfully complete them.

Earth can be hard at times, and some things that happen can make us cry. The hard times can be special opportunities to help us build our characters, to grow in virtue, to become spiritually stronger, and to appreciate God and other people more. Our difficult experiences can help us understand how other people think and feel who have gone through the same hard times we are going through. If we "walk in their shoes" for a while, we will understand how we can be of service to others who have the same problems.

God desires that we help and love each other while we live on earth. If we do that, it makes God very happy, and it makes everyone in Heaven very happy too. If we are loving and caring people, after we die and we go back to live with God in Heaven again, we will be proud of the life and the time we spent on earth.

When God sent us off to live on earth, He hoped that we would remember to pray and talk to Him every day. He hoped that we would stay close to Him and ask for His help about everything. God knew that earth would be way too hard on us if we did not continually ask Him to lend a hand. If we do ask God to help us, He will tell our angels to give us lots of extra assistance.

Remember to thank God daily for everything in your life when you pray to Him; if you do, you will start to see all the blessings and tender loving care God has been giving you. You will never feel alone and feel very loved.

Even though sometimes things can cause us to cry, we can still be happy and feel okay about it if we ask God to help us. God answers all prayers, but sometimes His answers are different from what we want. This is because God knows what is best for us. God isn't being mean. He knows when it'll take something different from what we asked for to complete successfully that special plan we made with Him before we came to earth. Sometimes our prayers take longer to get answered than we'd like, so we need to be a little patient with God and to trust Him and His perfect timing. God knows everything about you—even how many hairs you have on your little head!

Finding Your Specific Purpose

As your children get older, they may want more answers and direction about what they should be specifically doing with their lives—

what career path they should take, for instance. Here are some child-like explanations that you can use if this question arises.

God gave everyone talents and abilities to use as good clues to help you know what you should be doing in your life when you get here. For example, you may be especially talented at sports, music, dancing, art, math, writing, or science. You may be very good at fixing cars, growing plants, creating or fixing mechanical gadgets, using computers, working with electronics, building things, or listening to people's problems. Strong interests in a few of these things and being good at them can be great clues to your career path.

Many times our accidents, illnesses, and hardships are part of the plan that we bravely and courageously made with God before we came down to earth too. This could be because we wanted to learn something important from it or because we hoped others around us would benefit from it. The hardships that we see people we love going through in life can be a vital clue in finding your own life's purpose too. Many times other people's hardships and sufferings will prompt us to move into a certain career or direction to help others. For instance, if someone we love has cancer, we may want to go into cancer research or became a doctor, nurse, or hospice worker because of it.

We get to choose our parents from our soul group families in Heaven who we believe will be the best ones to help us accomplish our learning lessons and our missions. For example, you may have possibly chosen a parent who has diabetes so that you would be afflicted with the diabetes gene. You may have chosen to do this in the hopes that your illness may touch others' hearts to find a cure. Or the reason may be to give your parents the chance to bring out the nurturing side in them. You may have chosen a musician to be your parent because you wanted to be a musician to bring joy to the world through your talent. Our lives on earth are meant to benefit others as well as ourselves.

If you notice what you are excited or passionate about, along with asking God to guide you, you can find out more about your specific purpose in life. If you ask God to show you what He wants you to do with your life, it will make Him very pleased and He will give you a lot of good clues and a lot of extra help too. So just ask God and be on the lookout for His clues.

Explaining Death—for Young Children

When a death occurs and you want to explain it in a physical and spiritual way to a young child, you might want to say to that child that when someone has died his or her body doesn't work anymore, but the spirit inside of that body flew up to Heaven to live with God. This will help the little child to understand that something obvious has changed about the physical aspect of the person's body, but also it suggests that there is another form of life in case they see the spirit later.

A simple example is about a pet that you can also use to explain what happens when a person dies. Let's imagine, for example, that your child's pet dog Spotty dies, and you want to explain death to your child. You might say something like this: "Spotty's body died. Spotty's body doesn't work anymore, but Spotty had a spirit inside him that does still work. Spotty's spirit looks like Spotty, and it has a lot of white light.

"When Spotty died his spirit flew out of his body right up to Heaven to live with God. Heaven is a really fun and happy place where he can play and run, and Spotty is very happy there being with God. Spotty doesn't hurt in Heaven.

"Spotty can see and hear you from Heaven so that you can still talk to him even if you can't see him. Sometimes Spotty's spirit may fly down from Heaven to play with you when you're playing or sleeping. So if you see or hear Spotty tell me."

I recognize that this example about a dog's spirit may seem a little peculiar and even a bit far out to some who are reading this and who have never heard about pets visiting us from the afterlife. However, the spirits of pets often come back to visit their beloved owners. I personally have experienced three of my own pets (two dogs and a cockatiel) visiting me from the afterlife, which brought me an enormous amount of comfort. And I thank God for these visits. There is an amazing story in this book called "Smokey and the Bandit" (see p. 149) about a child's afterlife encounters with the family's pet dog. If you are looking for more pet stories of afterlife visits, there are more in my book, *God's Gift of Love: After-Death Communications.*

Explaining Death and Physical vs. Spiritual Bodies— for Older Children

When you are going to explain death or an impending death to an older child, just tell them the simple, plain facts about what caused the death or what will be causing the death. Then you could share the following information with them, which includes the Circle of Life:

Before we came to earth, we all lived happily with God in Heaven. We were spirits then with perfect spirit bodies. We could fly and walk through walls. Spirits look like people with a lot of white light. Our spirits are invisible energy, and they never hurt and they never get sick or die. Spirits live forever.

God explained that coming to earth for a little while would be important for us to do for our souls' growth. That if we volunteered to come to earth to live for a little while, that we'd need a physical body to wear while we lived there. We got to choose with God what our human bodies would look like and what the color of our skin, hair, and eyes would be. Some brave spirits even decided to choose bodies that wouldn't be perfect. Our physical bodies are like a costume that we wear over our spiritual bodies. We can't see our spirits that are hidden under our bodies though. When we have a physical body, we can't fly and walk through walls as we could when we were spirits in Heaven. When we have a body, we can get hurt and sick, and one day will die.

When we die, our bodies do not work anymore, but our spirits still do. When we die, it is okay because then we are no longer sick, nor do we have any pain. When we die, our spirits (this happens to animals and pets too) pop right out of our physical bodies, and they are perfect again. Our spirits can fly again, and we get to fly straight back to God in Heaven. God is so happy to have us back with Him that He hugs and kisses us when we get there. God has a big party for us. All His angels and our family, friends, and pets who died before us and are in Heaven are at the big party. When we die, we are so happy to be back in Heaven to be with God again because God, who is everybody's daddy, loves us the best.

Our loved ones in Heaven still get to see and hear us, and sometimes they will visit us while we are awake or in our dreams to let us know they love us and watch over us.

Explaining a Body at a Funeral

If you decide to take your young child to a funeral, please explain what death is and what a spirit looks like (see "Explaining Death and Physical vs. Spiritual Bodies" on p. 218). Tell your child that it's just his or her body in the coffin or box, but that the loved one's spirit won't be in it. The spirit has flown up to Heaven and gets to fly back and forth from Heaven from time to time. This'll help the child understand why the spirit of the person at his or her own funeral or at a later date might be seen.

There is a wonderful story (see p. 28) in this book called "Quit Blowing Spit," wherein little three-year-old Trevor wisely told his very shocked mother that when they go to the funeral of his baby brother, Tyler, that Tyler won't be in the box, it's just his body. Trevor's mother realized that Tyler's little spirit gave Trevor that astute and comforting information.

What Does God Look Like?

If your child asks what God looks like, explain in accordance with your particular belief system. One suggestion that may help your child visualize God as a personal being would be to explain that God looks like a big man with a whole lot of bright light, like the sun. (There are many children's books on the market in traditional and religious bookstores that depict pictures of a personal being as God or Jesus. Pictures can help your child visualize a tangible God even more so than words can convey.)

You can explain to him or her that God is everybody's daddy, loves us the best and is our best friend. God's heart is filled with all the love in the world for us. God really loves it when we talk to Him and pray to Him every day. God misses us when we forget to talk to Him.

What Is Heaven?—for Young Children

If your young child asks what Heaven is, you could say that Heaven is a beautiful and fun place where God, Jesus, your Creator (or whatever name you use to refer to your Divine Source) lives. Angels live there and so do the spirits of people and pets we know and love who have died. In Heaven we can fly. Heaven has houses, playgrounds, gardens, oceans, mountains, and friendly animals. There are sports, music, dancing, singing, drawing, and coloring. Children and adults get to play, learn, and have fun jobs. In Heaven we get kisses and hugs from God. Everyone is happy there and nobody cries, hurts, or dies in Heaven. Sometimes we can see Heaven in our dreams.

What Is Heaven Like?—for Older Children

God wanted to share His beautiful home called Heaven with us because He loves us so very much and wanted us to be happy forever

living there with Him. So God created all of us to be spirit/souls living with Him in Heaven. At one time, everyone used to live in
Heaven with God before we came down to earth to live. We are all
brothers and sisters, even though we don't all live together in the
same house on earth and even though we live in many different
countries and speak many different languages. God is everyone's
daddy, and we are all His kids.

Heaven is a beautiful paradise where God lives with His angels
and where good spirits live—like our family, friends, and pets—that
have died. Heaven is an invisible and spiritual dimension (place)
that human beings usually cannot see until after we die. Sometimes
we get to visit Heaven in our dreams. Spirits live in houses and get to
do things such as swim in the ocean, play sports, sing, dance, play
musical instruments, do artwork, build things, play with friends,
family, animals, pets, and angels, and fly to the moon and stars. Spirits still get to learn and teach in Heaven too. There are so many fun
things to do in Heaven!

Spirits and angels help each other in Heaven. They also help us
here on earth and watch over us. Spirits and angels have important
and fun jobs to do for God. They are very kind and love us very
much. Spirits in Heaven get hugged and kissed by God, who loves us
with His whole heart. Being in Heaven with God is the greatest
place to be and where our hearts long to be. We will be completely
happy forever in Heaven with God.

What Are Angels?

Explain to your child that God made the angels. Angels are spirits
that look like beautiful people and have lots of bright light. Many
times they have wings on their backs and they can fly. The angels
work for God. God is their boss and their daddy too. God gives His
angels lots of jobs to do. Some of their jobs are to protect us, watch
over us, guide us, and pray to God for us. The angels love us very

much. They are our helpers and friends and think of us as their brothers and sisters. Our angels are always around us. Most of the time we can't see our angels. Sometimes they will surprise us and show us they are around us. Sometimes people who die can look like angels. (You can refer to many pictures of angels in books on the market and online on the Internet so that your children can visualize them.)

Hell, Purgatory, and the Lower Realms

I suggest that you wait until your child reaches school age before you talk to him or her about these realms using your own belief system on these concepts. If you are seeking more in-depth information on an adult level for yourself on the topics of Heaven, hell, the other waiting place/purgatory, missions, blueprints of our lives, soul group families, angels unawares, and prophetic insights, I highly recommend reading the book *Glimpses of Heaven* by Sunni Welles.

Why Did My Loved One Have to Die?

Although this entire chapter is important to read to get the most complete information to answer your children's many questions, the previous sections on "The Purpose of Coming to Earth" (see p. 214) and "Explaining Death and Physical vs. Spiritual Bodies" (see p. 218) give specific reasons why. You can reiterate that our real and lasting permanent home is Heaven. Everyone who comes to earth is only meant to be here for a short time. It is like going to summer school. The best and most wonderful place to be is Heaven, and we will be together there again. For uplifting and hopeful sections to go along with this information, please refer to "Explaining Afterlife Visits" (see p. 231) and also "Contacting the Loved One or Pet" (see p. 232).

Why Did My Pet Have to Die?

A different explanation is required for our pets. Pets have spiritual bodies, but not souls, so they have no need for soul growth.

Our pets were created by God and lived in Heaven with God before they came to earth. God sends us pets to be our special friends, to teach us about loving without any conditions, and to love and take care of them. But all animals and people are the happiest when they live in Heaven, where there is all love, no pain or hunger or sadness. It is a place where they can freely play all the time. Only God knows when it is the right time for our pets to go back to Heaven to live and play again, but one day we will get to play with our pets in Heaven for as often and as long as we like. In the meantime, our family, friends, and angels in Heaven take good care of our pets. We can still talk to our pets because they can still see and hear us even if we can't see them.

Grief and Emotions

Children's Tears

You can explain to your child that even though our brothers, sisters, grandparents, moms, dads, uncles, aunts, cousins, friends, and pets are so happy to be back in Heaven with God again, the rest of us who are still on earth miss them, and we may feel very sad and cry a lot. It is normal to cry and feel sad. In fact it is a good thing to cry when we are sad. Crying is a healthy release for the pain we are feeling. As parents, remember that a hug is so appreciated by our children when they are crying. It shows them that it is okay to cry and that we love them. We want to comfort them, and we care about their feelings and pain; they are just as important as the loved ones who have departed. It can also help to open up a dialogue.

Adults' Tears

As a wise Native American Indian once noted in 1876, "The soul would have no rainbow if the eyes had no tears." As parents, understand that expressing feelings is essential in order to release and work through the pain we are feeling. If you are feeling sad and want to cry, allow yourself to cry in front of your children too so that they will know it is socially acceptable to cry. Then they will not feel embarrassed or weak if they do cry when in front of others or when alone. You will be teaching them a valuable lifelong lesson that will serve them well if you do. Although crying is often thought of as being weak, you will notice that many strong athletes will cry whether or not they have won or lost a championship game. A humorous line about crying spoken by the actor Tom Hanks is heard in the popular movie *A League of Their Own*: "There's no crying in baseball!" However, in real life there *is* crying in sorrow, and it has an invaluable and therapeutic effect. God created tears for a reason.

Anger, Forgiveness, and Guilt

It is important to talk or write about any anger we may be feeling, with the ultimate goal of someday forgiving. Forgiving does not mean condoning someone's actions. Forgiving just means letting go of the anger, the resentment, and the agitated and relentless desire to get revenge. Holding on to anger and resentments are poisons to our systems and will prevent us from being happy and at peace. Anger keeps us from moving forward by continually reliving the unhappy past and may cause us to do harm to others and to ourselves. Forgiveness is a gift we give to ourselves and to others on earth as well as in the afterlife. When we forgive someone who has died, that person really appreciates it. A huge burden will be lifted from your heart too. Ask God to help you forgive if you are having trouble with this. God wants you to forgive, to go forward in life, and to live in peace.

Forgive yourself too. Are you feeling guilty and having a hard time forgiving yourself for past unkindnesses or neglectfulness toward someone who has passed over? Forgiving yourself is just as important as forgiving others. When spirits are back in Heaven with God, they automatically forgive us for any wrongs we may have done to them intentionally or unintentionally. Forgiveness is a Godly virtue, and it is part of what being in Heaven is about. Nobody holds grudges in Heaven, nor do they hold onto anger. Anger and grudges are only human emotions, not heavenly spiritual emotions. Those living in Heaven are filled with God's light and love, so they feel complete peace and love.

They also get to view everything from their past from a spiritual learning perspective. They finally understand why they did the things that they did on earth. They also recognize why we did the things that we did that may have negatively had an inpact on them. There is complete knowledge, compassion, empathy, and understanding toward us that they may not have been able to feel fully before when living in a human body. They now know all the reasons why, and they can read our hearts. And they forgive us without even asking.

If you are feeling guilty and are sorry for anything you may have done to hurt them, then just say it or write it to them in a letter. Tell God you are sorry also, and that will be the end of it. You are forgiven. Believe it and you will be able to live a burdensome-free life about those past issues. They want you to let go of your guilt, as does God. They want you to stop beating yourself up. It is destructive to do so. They want you to go forward refreshed, renewed, and relieved and able to reinvest in life with joy in your heart. Spirits in Heaven want the very best for us. They want us to be the best that we can be.

Anger at God over a Death

It is not unusual for adults and children to feel anger at God over the death of someone they love. We may feel angry because that person had to suffer or had to leave us and now we are suffering. We may wonder why a loving God did not intervene to save that person's life as we had so fervently prayed for. We may even lose our faith over it. Your child may wonder why God would be so mean and so unfair.

If we are not aware that each soul created in Heaven volunteers to come to earth to live temporarily and that most people know ahead of time how they are going to die and agree to this for the soul's growth, it is easy to assume that God is mean and is punishing us. Please explain to your child that most deaths were part of the special agreement the person made with God ahead of time when he or she was living in Heaven. All plans are about advancing the soul's spiritual growth and the growth of those around us to bring us closer to God and to higher realms in Heaven even if there is temporary suffering involved. God respects and honors those plans that have been agreed upon prior to coming to earth. He keeps His promises. When we return to Heaven, we do not care about past sufferings. We are just so happy to be in Heaven and pleased with the accomplishment of our soul's growth if we successfully completed our mission. (For a more in-depth explanation, please refer to the section called "The Purpose of Coming to Earth" on p. 214).

Remind your child that we cannot know everything that God knows. We will eventually understand more about it when we get to ask God in person.

Holding anger toward God will only end up making you feel even more miserable. Your anger may cause you to separate yourself from your most loving Source, where peace, comfort, and healing await you. The longer you hold on to your anger at God, the longer it will take you to heal and to feel happy again. Healing does not take place without God's involvement whether you are consciously aware of this fact or not.

Gently suggest to your children to try to forgive God for things they do not understand right now. Remind them that God always forgives them when they ask Him to, so they should try to forgive God. If they do and if they trust that God knows best and really loves them and that there was a really good spiritual reason for what happened, they will be able to live more peace-filled lives during the most difficult of times. They will have the benefit of feeling close to God again, which is a place that our hearts long to be. Remind them that they can ask God to heal their hearts so that they can smile again. He wants them to.

Depression

While it is normal to feel sad, feel lonely, and have a temporary mild depression after someone we love dies, the loss can sometimes trigger a severe and persistent clinical depression that will need treatment from a professional. Watch for this when it comes to your child's grief or your own. This type of depression must not be ignored.

Guilty Feeling Happy

I have met so many people who felt guilty if they found themselves laughing or smiling again after the loss of a loved one. They somehow felt that experiencing moments of joy was being disrespectful, disloyal, or hurtful to their departed loved ones' feelings. They worried that their loved ones might think they have forgotten about them, were not affected by the loss, or were no longer loved by them if they found happiness again.

They felt very conflicted if they found themselves able to laugh and not think about their departed loved ones 24/7. But if you've read some of the blissful NDEs in this book and on the market, you can better understand how awesome Heaven is for our loved ones who are residing there and how happy they are. Doesn't it seem a bit strange and one-sided to think that they'd want you to be so miserable when they're enjoying paradise? Doesn't it seem logical that loved ones who love you would want you not only to celebrate for them but to be happy too? When we truly love someone, we sincerely want the loved one's happiness, don't we? Think about it. If the roles were reversed, if you were so ecstatic about being back home in Heaven, would you want your loved ones back on earth to be suffering? Of course not! It'd make you so pleased and relieved to see them happy. Well, this is the way your loved one feels about you. They want you to feel their joy, and they want you to reinvest in life and live it to the fullest. They want you to know that you'll be to-gether spirit-to-spirit again, as the stories in this book show. In the meantime, they want you to complete successfully your own learning experiences and missions on earth and the reason why you temporar-ily left Heaven to come here. They'll be with you helping you with your life's purpose all along the way, like an angel on your shoulder.

The son of one of the contributors and a member of Prayer Wave was murdered. She explained that as a grieving mother she found herself crying all the time. One night her son visited her in a dream and told her that he was so happy and loved it where he was living now. He took her to Heaven and showed her how beautiful and awe-some it was, but the only thing that made him sad was seeing his family cry all the time. He told her that they would be together again someday, but until then to be happy for him.

Isn't this a message from beyond for all of us? Be happy for them and don't feel guilty if you're living a joyful life. They dearly desire this for you. Seeing you happy gives them a greater sense of gratifica-tion and enjoyment. Being happy doesn't mean that we've forgotten about them. They know this. They know they forever live in our hearts. They also know it's important and necessary to concentrate on the living too. Remember to treasure the ones who are still living with you on earth, and don't neglect them. They still need you.

Never feel guilty for feeling and spreading joy. When you are happy, you spread happiness to others and make our world a better place for all who come in contact with you. Smile and the world smiles with you—even your loved ones too!

Recovering from Grief

Hugs and Special Comforters

Your child may not mention this, but he or she may really miss being hugged and touching the loved one. Hugging your children when they are feeling sad will comfort them (and you) immensely.

You could also make your child a special hug pillow with the loved one's image on the cover. A hug pillow, a special stuffed animal, a quilt, or a toy will give your child something tangible to hold on to for the important purposes of expressing love and affection and for feeling comforted. You can make a snuggly quilt out of the clothes of your loved one. Simply sew the clothes on top of a quilt or make a new quilt consisting of only his or her clothing. The closeness of having the loved one's clothes next to the child will be very soothing.

Talking About the Loved One

It is so necessary to talk about the people we miss and to talk about our sadness and our feelings too. It is also soul healing to laugh, to talk about them, and to remember the happy times we had with them. They listen in and laugh with us. They may even let you know that they are there! Talk to your children about the happy times that you all had with their loved ones. Celebrate their life. It will help bring you all closer.

The Dead See and Hear Us

Over the years, as a Facilitator of Spiritual Bereavement Recovery, I have observed time and again that our loved ones in Heaven continue to see us and can hear our words and thoughts of them. The validating stories in this book will help confirm that to you. Your conversations, your thoughts, and your words to your loved ones in Heaven go directly to them. Many times they will try to let us know they have heard us by the "signs" they give us. Many of my clients tell me they routinely talk to their departed loves ones. So do I! Even though most of the time it is a one-way conversation, it is extremely comforting to do so. So continue to talk to them!

Saying Good-bye and Hello

From my personal spiritual experiences, conversations, and work with the bereaved since 1998, I have learned that our loved ones in Heaven continue to be an ongoing part of our lives. There is no end to the spiritual connection and relationship we have with those who went on to Heaven before us. Because of this, I always like to suggest that when we say or write a good-bye letter that we are saying good-bye to the physical person, but at the same time saying hello to the new spiritual relationship that we are now going to have with that person—if we desire to continue the relationship. You may want to mention this to your child.

If you didn't get a chance to say good-bye, writing a good-bye/ hello letter to your loved one will give you the opportunity to express those special unspoken treasured words. It'll help give you a sense of completion.

Letters to the Departed

We can write the loved one letters, and we can also read our letters out loud to them expressing all our thoughts and feelings. It may be helpful to have a photo of the loved one in front of your child when he or she writes a personal letter to the loved one. In addition to writing positive letters of love, thanks, and expressions of I miss you to the one we are missing, if your child has any anger, guilt, regrets, or other negative feelings, the letter to the loved one is a beneficial way to express, release, and purge those negative feelings from his or her system. Even though the loved one can hear the thoughts and words directed to him or her, reading the letter out loud to the loved one gives a heightened sense of that person's presence around us, quietly listening to us. Your child could also save the written letters in a special decorated box dedicated to the loved one, with the loved one's name written on it. The child can save them in a private album and can write a letter anytime he or she has something to say to the loved one.

Drawing Pictures

Children derive a great deal of benefit from drawing pictures. This helps them express their innermost feelings that they may not be able to verbalize to anyone. Gently encourage this and make available the art supplies in case they would like to do this.

Breaking the Cycle of Grief

It takes time to get used to the new normal after a loved one dies. The future may seem bleak and empty, because in addition to the sadness and longing, we may believe that we will never be happy again. We may feel that life no longer holds any meaning for us. I have met many parents and others who were bereaved who felt this way at first. However, over time they were very pleasantly surprised to find that they could actually smile, laugh, and be happy again. Part of this happiness was due to the blessing of receiving afterlife contacts and signs, which gave their children and them the positive reinforcement that their loved ones were still an ongoing part of their lives—even though they have a heavenly address now.

To help break the cycle of grief and to bring you moments of joy, I highly recommend taking a minivacation with your children. Seeing new places and doing new things can be very therapeutic and can temporarily take you and your children's minds off your loss and pain. You will all see that it is very possible to have some fun in your lives—which is what your minds, bodies, and spirits especially need at this time. Ask the loved ones to come along and enjoy the vacation with you! They may even find a fun and creative way to let you know that they are with you enjoying the vacation too! They are now able to travel with you anywhere you go. They no longer have any physical limitations. How exciting for them.

Adults and children can join groups dedicated to activities and hobbies that they enjoy. They can volunteer to be in service for special causes that speak to their hearts. All these things will help them take their minds off themselves and to positively reinvest in life.

Explaining Afterlife Visits

Let your child know that at times God allows people and pets we love and miss, who have died and are living in Heaven, to fly back to earth to show us they are around us and to let us know that they continue to see and hear us. All children are very special to God, and some children are able at times to see the visiting spirits of people or pets we love who have died, as the stories in this book emphatically demonstrate. When they do fly back to visit us, they may play with us, help us, guide us gently, or watch over us as our angels do. They may fly through doors, windows, walls, and out of mirrors or be near the ceiling or in the corner of the room when they come to visit. And it is a lot of fun for them. Sometimes they will visit us when we are sleeping and dreaming. Sometimes adults can see them too. Ask your child to let you know if he or she ever sees the spirit of a loved one or any spirits at all. The visits may be so routine for your child that he or she may not even think of telling you about them, unless you specifically ask.

Contacting the Loved One or Pet—for Younger Children

If your young child wants to contact a loved one or pet, one helpful idea would be to ask your child to draw a picture for the loved one or you could write the loved one a letter for your child. You could attach the drawing or the letter to a balloon and together release it into the sky and watch it ascend up to Heaven. Or you could just release a balloon. Sometimes children will report actually seeing the loved ones catch the balloons that they have sent up to them.

One mother told me that her four-year-old child reported that when he released a balloon for his little baby brother in Heaven, he saw his little brother grab the balloon, and his brother said that he was taking it to show it off to the other babies in Heaven!

For Older Children

Our prayers are very powerful when it comes to receiving afterlife contacts. Your child can pray to God to ask to receive a comforting visit from the loved one. Many times God will answer those prayers by sending our loved ones to us to turn our sorrow into joy and to help us heal from the pain of grief. The loved one may come to your child in an apparition, in dreams, or may use other types of comforting afterlife signs indicating their presence. For adults wanting to receive an afterlife contact, pray to God to receive one, then state something specific to your loved one that you would recognize as a sign from the loved one, for example, a butterfly. As I mentioned in chapter 1, the ADC researchers, Judith and Bill Guggenheim, state that it is estimated that 60–120 million Americans have had one or more (spontaneous and direct) ADC experiences. So ADCs are very common occurrences.

If you or your child desire a pleasant dream visit from your loved one and are wondering how to get one, ask God to allow them to come to you in your dreams and ask God to protect you while you sleep. Then before drifting off to sleep, talk to your loved one and visualize being together in a place that you would both enjoy, on vacation, for instance. Keep a pad and pen near your bed to record any bits of your dream before you fully wake up.

Suicides and Afterlife Visits

It is crucial to seek help if one is feeling suicidal. God does not want us to take our own lives. He wants us to use our precious gift of life as an opportunity to complete our lessons and earthly missions successfully for important soul growth. However, God knows better than anyone that some people are suffering with brain chemical imbalances. If your loved one was afflicted with this illness, and has chosen to take their own life because of it, God understands the circumstances and does not hold that person responsible for his or her actions.

Mercifully, many times people who have committed suicide for whatever reason, will visit us later on from the afterlife to show us that they are okay now and in God's light. There is no need to continue to worry about them. These afterlife visits are a gift from God's heart to comfort yours.

Ongoing Spiritual Relationships

Praying for the Dead

Our prayers are very helpful to those souls who are having a hard time forgiving themselves before God for things they may have done while on earth that they are ashamed of and are now sorry for. Your prayers are invaluable in this regard and are greatly appreciated by them. Prayers really do make a difference. Sometimes they will find a way to thank you for your prayers on their behalf.

They Never Forget Us

Please let your child know that our loved ones in Heaven never forget about us, and they love us forever. They are also around us a lot trying to help us in our lives, like our angels. They want us to still have fun and be happy because they are happy. They look forward to the day when we are all back together in Heaven with them. But we have to wait our turn to go back to Heaven because only God knows when it is the right time to call us back.

Remembering and Celebrating

Planting a tree or working on a memorial garden dedicated to the loved one is a visible way to do something positive in the loved one's memory. Establishing a scholarship in his or her name is another. You can give to a cause or a charity that helps others in your loved one's name. For instance, if your loved one passed from cancer, heart disease, Lou Gehrig's disease, diabetes, AIDS, or multiple sclerosis, for instance, giving to a particular charity to help with research and education would be a very constructive and worthwhile endeavor in which to honor that person. We can honor our loved one by volunteering to help others who are suffering from the same illness or anyone who is in need.

Anniversaries and Birthdays

On these sensitive and emotional annual occasions, we can light candles and meditate about them. We can gather together to pray for them or have a Mass of prayers said for them. We can release balloons in their honor. We can gather together at their favorite restaurants, recreation areas, or vacation spots and share fond memories of them. We can celebrate their earth birthdays with birthday cakes. We can bring out videos and photo albums and reminisce about the fun times. We can physically or financially do something for the needy on that day.

Bereavement Support

Adult Books on Grief

While *Heaven Talks to Children* concentrates on children's grief, adults also need help when it comes to recovering from grief. What adults learn about grief healing and recovery can be used to make a positive impact on their children. Some of the suggestions I have given you in this book for your children are applicable to you too.

While there are grief resources listed in the back of this book, one of my favorite books for adults that I highly recommend for its wisdom and practical advice on healing from grief is *Love Lives On* by Louis LaGrand, Ph.D. Dr. LaGrand is a friend of mine and I greatly admire his compassion and heartfelt desire to help the bereaved. He is the author of eight books and numerous articles and is known worldwide for his research on the extraordinary experiences of the bereaved (ADC phenomena) and its healing effects.

God Is the Best Healer

In my years of spiritual bereavement recovery work with hundreds of people since 1998, I have observed that those who have a close relationship with God, and who turn to God in their time of sorrow, seem to find acceptance, peace, and happiness, and they may heal faster than those who do not seek out God's help. He is your most powerful ally and resource to help you recover from your grief. Tap into the heavenly divine pool of healing and love that is always available and waiting for you. God wants to heal you with His tender loving care, but He respectfully waits to be asked.

On a personal note, four years after my dad passed, my mother also passed. There was a deep pain and longing in my heart from losing the physical presence of my last surviving parent. However, I believed that God, my dad, and my mother wanted me to be happy again. I certainly longed to be happy again, so I turned to God and asked specifically for that. I asked Jesus to replace my heart's sorrow with His joy. These were the only words that I could barely utter to God in my time of deep grief and sorrow. I would say this prayer every time I felt the pain wash over me. I began to notice that the pain was beginning to lessen. After two weeks of saying this specific prayer, a miracle happened. The pain in my heart suddenly left me. Yes, I still missed my mother, but I was no longer in pain. God had blessed me with many afterlife signs from my mother. Joy now actually replaced my sorrow, which is what I had asked for.

I highly recommend praying to God (by whatever name you lovingly refer to your Creator or Divine Source) to replace your heart's sorrow with His joy. When we pray, God really does listen and will try to help all His "kids" (adults and children) whom He loves and dearly cares about. Ask your child to pray to God to help him or her to feel better and to be happy again. You and your child will be amazed at how comforting and healing your prayers to God can be during this very sorrowful time in your lives. I have personally found that prayer trumps everything when it comes to grief healing, and over the years, as a founder of an Internet prayer group, I have seen so many others be healed through prayer to God.

Online Grief and Prayer Support

If you are grieving and looking for uplifting online bereavement support, including prayers on your behalf to receive a comforting after-death sign from your loved one, please visit my nondenominational message board at my Prayer Wave for After-Death Communication website at www.christineduminiak.com. It is the most loving and healing place on the Internet filled with the most beautiful and compassionate-hearted people who understand your pain because they have been there too. Their powerful prayers really do touch God's heart, and we feel His healing presence with us.

Final Thoughts About Your Children's Welfare

Children are our purest and most treasured gift temporarily on loan to us from God. This may be for one second, one day, or one hundred years. They are part of our heavenly soul group family. We don't know what their souls' plans are with God. We don't own them. God entrusts them in our care for an unspecified period of time while they learn their lessons and complete their missions on earth. While they are in our care, we are expected to love them, guide them, listen to them, respect them, and nurture them in all ways—including spiritual ways. Teach them about God. Let them know how special they are to you and to God, their Heavenly Daddy, and how they can go to Him at anytime about anything. He loves it when they do. Be a shining example and a moral compass for your children. God will bless you for doing so.

When children share their sacred supernatural experiences with us, it is very important that we believe, accept, and safely guide them. However, all children should be children first and live normal balanced lives. They should not be placed on a pedestal if they have a spiritual gift, nor should they be condemned because of fears or prejudices, which I have addressed in chapter 5. Even though thousands of parents are reporting that their children can see dead people, it has been only relatively recently that children's spiritual gifts and abilities have been talked about in the mainstream media and on national TV shows in the United States.

Since there are many children and adult skeptics who do not yet understand, embrace, or believe in supernatural gifts or afterlife visits, it would be wise if you and your children bring this topic up cautiously to people whom you trust and whom you both feel safe with. Your child may find that some very close friends will think it is cool that they are seeing spirits, while others may freak out. Some may even make fun of your child. Some may even share that they are seeing spirits too and will be relieved to hear that they are not alone. If any of your child's friends have this gift, you may want to give their parents a copy of this book. If your child has this ability, you may want to give his or her teachers and other interested professionals whom your child interacts with a copy of this book to bring more awareness and understanding about this spiritual ability. By their reading these one hundred-plus children's stories, I believe there will be a cumulative and mind-opening effect on those who have not been previously exposed to this phenomenon.

As parents, by carefully nurturing this wonderful facet of your child's God-given spiritual attributes, you will be the beneficiary of knowing that your loved ones are okay in Heaven and continue to be an important spiritual part of your life till you meet again. By teaching your child to ask God to be in service to Him with his or her gift, your child will start to see the greater good that this gift can bring about for God's holy purposes and Divine plan.

May God bless you and your dear children.

Recommended Reading and Other Sources

Bowman, Donna. *The Walking Wounded.* Scotts Valley, CA: Create-Space, 2008.

Brinkley, Dannion, and Paul Perry. *Saved by the Light.* New York: Harper Paperbacks, 1994.

Clark, Nancy. *Hear His Voice.* Frederick, MD.: Publish America, 2005.

Cruz, Joan. *Mysteries Marvels Miracles: In the Lives of the Saints.* Rockford, IL: Tan Books, 1997.

Duminiak, Christine. *God's Gift of Love: After-Death Communications.* Philadelphia, PA: Xlibris, 2003.

Eadie, Betty. *Embraced by the Light.* Placerville, CA: Gold Leaf Press, 1992.

Edward, John. *One Last Time.* New York: Berkley, 1998.

Gellman, Rabbi Marc, and Msgr. Thomas Hartman. *Religion for Dummies.* New York: Wiley, 2003.

Guggenheim, Will, and Judith Guggenheim. *Hello From Heaven.* New York: Bantam, 1996.

Hooper, John. *"Dialogue with the Dead Is Feasible, Vatican Spokesman Says."* London Observer Service. January 1997.

Ignatius, Bro. Paul. *Seven Types of Ghosts: A Catholic, Biblical Perspective.* Order of the Legion of St. Michael, OSWC, 2001.

James, John, Russell Friedman, and Leslie Matthews. *When Children Grieve.* New York: HarperCollins, 2001.

Kreeft, Peter. *Angels (and Demons): What Do We Really Know About Them?.* Ft. Collins, CO: Ignatius Press, 1995.

Kübler-Ross, Elisabeth. *On Life After Death*. Berkeley, CA: Celestial Arts, 1991.

LaGrand, Louis. *After Death Communications: Final Farewells*. St. Paul, MN: Llewellyn, 1997.

———. *Love Lives On*. New York: Berkley, 2006.

Lawson, Lee. *Visitations from the Afterlife*. New York: HarperCollins, 2000.

Moody, Raymond. *Life After Life*. New York: Bantam, 1979.

Morse, Melvin, and Paul Perry. *Closer to the Light*. New York: Villard Books, 1990.

———. *Transformed By The Light*. New York: Villard Books, 1992.

O'Connor, Joey. *Children and Grief*. Grand Rapids, MI: Fleming H. Revell, 2004.

Piper, Don. *90 Minutes in Heaven*. With Cecil Murphey. Grand Rapids, MI: Fleming H. Revell, 2004.

Schneider, Lisa. *Faith in the Departed*. (May 2005), www.beliefnet. com (accessed December 23, 2009).

Steiger, Brad, and Sherry Steiger. *Angels Over their Shoulders*. New York, NY: Ballantine Books, 1995.

Storm, Rev. Howard. *My Descent into Death: A Second Chance at Life*. New York, NY: Doubleday, 2005.

Treece, Patricia. *Apparitions of Modern Saints*. Ann Arbor, MI: Servant, 2001.

Underwood, Blair. *Before I Got Here*. New York: Atria Books, 2005.

Van Praagh, James. *Talking to Heaven*. New York: Dutton, 1997.

Varga, Josie, *Visits from Heaven*. Virginia Beach: 4th Dimension Press, 2009.

Welles, Sunni. *Glimpses of Heaven from the Angels Who Live There*. Philadelphia, PA: Xlibris, 2003.

About the Author

CHRISTINE DUMINIAK is a Certified Grief Recovery Specialist, an International Spiritual Bereavement Recovery Facilitator, and the founder and spiritual adviser of Prayer Wave for After-Death Communications—a nondenominational online grief support and prayer group with over five hundred members from twenty-one countries. Duminiak is a member of the Association for Death Education and Counseling and has been in the field of spiritual bereavement support since 1998. She is the author of *God's Gift of Love: After-Death Communications* and the creator and voice of the guided meditation CD titled *Meditation of God's Love and Healing: For Those Who Grieve.*

Duminiak is a frequent guest speaker in James Van Praagh's chat room. Her book and grief support and prayer group are recommended by James Van Praagh for grief support and understanding the afterlife.

Duminiak frequently speaks at The Learning Annex in New York City, to The Compassionate Friends, to Mothers Against Drunk Driving (MADD), to Rotary Clubs, to senior citizen groups, spirituality groups, to bereavement groups, and to the general public. She travels around the country giving seminars.

A Certified Reflexologist and a Certified Energy Healing Practitioner, Duminiak has volunteered her time and skills to hospice and cancer patients, for women in crisis pregnancies at shelters, and for women transitioning from substance abuse shelters.

Duminiak has been a featured expert guest on NBC 12 TV the *Arizona Midday* show in Phoenix; on NBC 10 TV's lifestyle and entertainment talk show *10!* in Philadelphia, Pennsylvania; on the news on NBC 10 TV; on the news on CBS 3 TV in Philadelphia; on *Tele-care TV*, Diocese of Rockville Centre, New York; on the *The God Squad* with Msgr. Tom Hartman and Rabbi Marc Gellman; on talk radio shows, including the nationally syndicated *Coast to Coast AM*; and in *The Philadelphia Inquirer*, *The Bucks County Courier-Times*, *The Arizona Republic*, *The East Valley Tribune* (Scottsdale), and *The Reporter in the Villages* (Florida).

Visit her website at www.christineduminiak.com. and e-mail her at christine@christineduminiak.com.